The tragedy of Mariam - Primary Source Edition

Elizabeth Cary, A C. 1878- Dunstan

Nabu Public Domain Reprints:

You are holding a reproduction of an original work published before 1923 that is in the public domain in the United States of America, and possibly other countries. You may freely copy and distribute this work as no entity (individual or corporate) has a copyright on the body of the work. This book may contain prior copyright references, and library stamps (as most of these works were scanned from library copies). These have been scanned and retained as part of the historical artifact.

This book may have occasional imperfections such as missing or blurred pages, poor pictures, errant marks, etc. that were either part of the original artifact, or were introduced by the scanning process. We believe this work is culturally important, and despite the imperfections, have elected to bring it back into print as part of our continuing commitment to the preservation of printed works worldwide. We appreciate your understanding of the imperfections in the preservation process, and hope you enjoy this valuable book.

a

PRINTED FOR THE MALONE SOCIETY BY
HORACE HART M.A. AT THE
OXFORD UNIVERSITY
PRESS

THE TRAGEDY OF MARIAM
1613

THE MALONE SOCIETY
REPRINTS
1914

This reprint of Lady Elizabeth Cary's *Tragedy of Mariam* has been prepared by A. C. Dunstan with the assistance of the General Editor.

July 1914.   W. W. Greg.

In the Register of the Stationers' Company is found the following entry:

17. Decembris [1612]

Entred for his copie vnder the handes of Sir George Bucke and master Richard Harison Warden A Booke called Mariamne The tragedie of the fayre Hawkins. Mariamne Quene of Iurye . . . . vj^d

[Arber's Transcript, iii. 508.]

The only known edition of the play here reprinted appeared in quarto with the date 1613. It bore the title: 'The Tragedie of Mariam, the faire Queene of Iewry', was printed by Thomas Creede for Richard Hawkins, and purported to be 'Written by that learned, vertuous, and truly noble Ladie, E. C.' It is to be noticed that the title-page affords no evidence that the authoress was a titled lady, though it does not necessarily imply the contrary. Copies of the quarto are not uncommon: there are three in the British Museum (162. c. 28, G. 11221 with title mutilated, C. 34. c. 9 wanting sig. I) and one in the Bodleian Library, all of which have been used in the preparation of the present reprint. Other copies are in the Dyce and Eton College Libraries; yet others were till recently in the Huth and Devonshire collections. A few slight variants have been observed. The quarto is printed in ordinary roman type of a body approximating to modern pica (20 ll. = 83 mm.).

All the copies mentioned above are (except where the contrary is stated) perfect so far as the bibliographical make up of the volume is concerned. But the Huth copy had the peculiarity of possessing an extra leaf which does not appear to be preserved in any other copy. This has recently gone to America and is for the moment unfortunately inaccessible. A full description of the copy will be found in the catalogue of 'The Huth Library' (1880, i. 263). After giving a transcript of the title it proceeds: 'A–I 2 in fours, besides a leaf marked A, which contains the verses to the authoress by her brother, and the dramatis personæ. This leaf should follow the title, and is frequently wanting.

v

It is directed by E. C. "To Dianaes Earthlie Depvtesse, and my worthy Sister, Mistris Elizabeth Carye". This copy has successively belonged to Mr. Bright, Mr. Holgate, and Mr. Corser.' It is to be observed that the leaf in question is an insertion, for the title forms the real A 1 of the volume.

The sonnet is not reproduced in the Catalogue, but the following communication from W. Carew Hazlitt appeared in 'Notes and Queries' for 9 Sept. 1865 (3 Ser. viii. 203): 'In examining some old books and MSS., for a different purpose, I came across a copy of *The Tragedy of Mariam, the Fair Queen of Jewry*, 1613, by Lady E. Carew, with a dedication which I never met with before in copies of this drama, as follows:—

"TO DIANAES
EARTHLIE DEPVTESSE,
and my worthy Sister, Mistris Elizabeth Carye.

"When cheerfull *Phœbus* his full course hath run,
His Sister's fainter Beams our harts doth cheere;
So your faire Brother is to mee the Sunne;
And you, his Sister, as my Moone appeare.

"You are my next belou'd, my second Friend,
For when my *Phœbus* absence makes it Night,
Whilst to th' *Antipodes* his beams do bend,
From you, my *Phœbe*, shines my second Light.

"Hee, like to Sol, cleare-sighted, constant, free,
You, Lvna-like, vnspotted, chast, deuine:
Hee shone on *Sicily*; you destin'd bee
T' illumine the now obscurde *Palestine*.
My first was consecrated to *Apollo*,
My second to Diana now shall follow.
E. C."'

This sonnet has often, as in the Huth Catalogue, been taken as gratulatory, that is, as addressed by a friend to the author, but in the absence of very strong evidence to the contrary we are bound to assume that the E. C. of the title-page and the E. C. of the sonnet refer to the same person.

All, therefore, that we are able immediately to infer is that the play was written by a lady whose initials were E. C. and who had a 'sister', Mistress Elizabeth Carye.

The fact that this extra leaf is only known to occur in one copy out of the many extant necessitates our supposing that only a very small portion of the edition ever had it. Either it is to be regarded as an insertion made in a few presentation copies only, or else as an afterthought added after the bulk of the edition had already been sold.

The play apparently figures in Rogers and Ley's list in 1656 as 'Mariamne Tragedy'. It will be observed that the form of the name here given agrees with that in the Stationers' Register—a curious coincidence. Though not used apparently by English writers at this time, it must have been known to a certain class of students as occurring in the Latin translations of Josephus: it is very rare in the Greek texts (see Niese's edition, Berlin, 1887). In 1656 likewise appeared Archer's catalogue, which contains the earliest ascription of our play: 'Mariame. T[ragedy]. Lady Eliz. Carew'. This was copied in Kirkman's lists; 'Mariame' becoming 'Mariam' in 1661, and 'Marian' in 1671. Since the name is spelt 'Carew' in the lists and 'Carey' in the dedication, the probability is that the former drew not from the latter, but from an inscription on the title of some copy in Archer's stock. Such old inscriptions are notoriously untrustworthy, and little authority can be attached to the statement in the lists.

It happens, however, to be perfectly correct. The play and the dedication were alike written by Lady Elizabeth Carey, or Cary, wife of Sir Henry Cary, who became Viscount Falkland in 1620. This appears from certain verses in the *Muses' Sacrifice* by John Davies of Hereford printed in 1612, but apparently not entered in the Stationers' Register. This work is dedicated to three ladies of whom one is 'Elizabeth, Lady Cary, (Wife of Sr Henry Cary:)', and to her the author writes:

> Thou mak'st Melpomen proud, and my heart great
> of such a Pupill, who, in Buskin fine,
> With Feete of State, dost make thy Muse to mete
> the scenes of Syracuse and Palestine.

These lines, taken in conjunction with the dedicatory sonnet already printed, afford satisfactory evidence that Davies is addressing the author of *Mariam*. That the later Viscountess Falkland is intended is also clear, for though there were several Lady Elizabeth Carys, and several Sir Henry Carys, there appears to have been but one Lady Elizabeth who was the wife of a Sir Henry. The material portions of Davies' dedication will be found printed at the end of the present introduction.

If Lady Elizabeth Cary was the E. C. of the sonnet, who was the Mistress Elizabeth Carey? Sir Henry Cary, later Viscount Falkland, had a sister Elizabeth, to whom the designation would of course apply, but it appears that she married Sir John Savile on 20 Nov. 1586, when the author of *Mariam* must have been still in her cradle. But Sir Henry also had a rather obscure brother Philip, who was knighted sometime between March 1605 and April 1609, and this Philip married a certain Elizabeth Bland of Carleton, Yorks. This lady must then have been the Mistress Elizabeth Cary to whom *Mariam* is dedicated.

The history therefore stands as follows. In the year 1600 Elizabeth Tanfield, only child of Lawrence Tanfield of Burford Priory, Oxford, later Sir Lawrence Tanfield and Lord Chief Baron of the Exchequer, became Lady Cary, wife of Sir Henry Cary, the son of a Hertfordshire knight. She was then about fifteen years old. Either just before or, more probably, soon after her marriage she wrote a play of which the scene is laid at Syracuse, and dedicated it to her husband. That was her first literary venture. Her second, *Mariam*, she dedicated to her namesake, the wife of her husband's brother, Philip. There is some reason to suppose that Philip was knighted in 1605, which would make the play the work of the first four years of the author's married life: it might safely be dated 1603-4. The date of Philip's marriage is unfortunately not known. The only difficulty is that the sonnet is to all appearances addressed to an unmarried woman. There is, however, nothing to prevent our supposing that Philip's bride, like Henry's, was still a child, and that it was some years before husband and wife lived together. Philip's eldest child was baptized in 1610, Henry's not before 1607. The authority for the dates given above will be found in the notes at the end of this introduction.

The play of *Mariam* must have circulated in manuscript among Lady Cary's friends, and for such manuscript copies, it is clear, the dedication was written, for by 1612 Philip's wife had ceased to be Mistress and had become Lady Cary. When in 1613 the play came to be printed the dedication as it stood was no longer correct. Had it been written in that year it must have been written very differently. Had it in that year been printed with a view to insertion in a few presentation copies, even then we might expect the heading at least to have been brought up to date. The play can hardly have been printed without the author's knowledge and at least acquiescence, for in view of the regular entry in the Stationers' Register and the licence by the Master of the Revels it is impossible to suppose that there was anything surreptitious about the publication. Perhaps the most probable conjecture is that after the play had been printed and part of the edition disposed of with the assent of the author, the dedication happened to come independently into the stationer's hands and that he printed and added it to the remainder of the stock without seeking further authority, and without troubling himself as to whether at that date it was, as it stood, correct. The fact that he utilized the back of the leaf for the addition of a list of dramatis personae suggests that he intended it as an integral portion of those copies in which it was inserted.

List of Doubtful Readings, &c.

N.B.—The following is primarily a list of those passages in which the reading of the original is open to question, and of those in which different copies of the original have been found to vary. It also includes a number of readings which are evident typographical blunders of the original, this being necessary as a defence of the accuracy of the reprint. It makes, however, no pretence of supplying a complete list of errors and corruptions, still less of offering any criticism or emendation. For the sake of greater clearness the readings are quoted in a slightly different manner from that adopted in the earlier Malone reprints. The mere repetition of a reading out of the text is equivalent to 'sic'. The three British Museum copies mentioned above are distinguished as A, B, and C respectively. It will be observed that the inner forme of sheet G is uncorrected in A, and the outer forme of sheet H in B and C, as also in the copy at Eton.

Arg. 4 daughrer (*properly* grand-daughter)
    6 reputia-|ted
  12 firſt (*properly* ſecond)
  13 ſecond (*properly* firſt)
  23 *Ioſophus*
  47 procured] *possibly* proeured
Text 12 (*line too short*)
  37 lowlyeſt (*read* louelyeſt?)
  49 maide (*read* minde)
  69 c.w. Th
  86 murthers (*read* murthrers)
  95 fain'd. (*read* fam'd.)
 127 *Mariam* (read *Herod*)
 136 *Nun:* (read *Mar:*)
     Alas
 138 If (*read* In *or* Of?)
 160 findes (*read* finde)
 187 leeke. (*read* ſeeke.)
 203 And part (*read* Apart?)
 225 diſcontent, (*read* diſcontents,)
 226 did (*read* doth?)
 261 fuſpitious (*read* fuſpitions)
 264 *Ioſephus* (read *Ioſephs?*)
 286 allyes (*read* all eyes)
 308 for
 310 *Contabarus*
 311 Earneſt
 335 Scœna
 351 do'es

 353 *Solleus.*
 366 not (*read* on?)
 373 home (*read* whom?)
 387 Scœna
 413 forfeited (*add* to *or* by?)
 439 beaſtes, ſwine,
     (*read* beaſtes ſwim,?)
 478 vowd. (*read* vow.)
 512-3 (*should be indented and followed by lead*)
 516 Of (*read* If?)
 521 chreefull,
 525 T'hother
 546 drawes nye] *possibly* drawesnye
 569 teach (*read* teach vs?)
 608 beſt (*read* leſt?)
 627 An d
 632 Scœna.
 634 *Babus.*
 673 operpaſt
 683 ſafely (*read* ſafety?)
 698 breath] *possibly* bre ath
 701 leare: (*read* feare:)
 710 gratitude *Conſt.* belieue
     (*read* gratitude. *Conſt.* Belieue)
 711 (*line too short*)
 728 llue, (*read* lie,)
 733 *Iulions*
 737 Phiſmony
 768 Your (*read* You?)

792 oath (*read* oaths?)
823 fortunes. (*read* fortunes,?)
848 expectation? (*read* exception??)
849 *Salom*, (*read* *Salome*,?)
877 loſt, (*read* loſſe,?)
931 I, I, they fight, (*presumably the corruption of a stage direction*)
933 Intru'd
934 late tofeare, (*read* late, I feare,?)
936 *Silleus* very (*read* *Silleus*. Very)
945 Sterne
948 ſo (*read* too?)
997 cane mak
1017 beautie,
1047 (*line too short*)
1061 her with you be (*read* here with you. Be?)
1068 done (*read* doom'd?)
1070 he (*read* we?)
1071 his (*read* our?)
1112 bides] *possibly* bides.
1126 (*belongs to Mariam*)
1142 Great] *possibly* Grear
1155 hypcorite:
1156 death] *possibly* d eath
1196 Alexanders (*read* *Alexandras*)
1262 *Mariam*? (*read* *Mariam*, how??)
1262, 1263 *Nutio*.
1273 Ioſualike
1281 griefe (*read* geeſe?)
1290 little, while (*read* little while,)
1297 Whoſe
1332 you (*read* your)
1339 *Salom* (*read* *Salome*?)
1343 them] *possibly* the m
1393 (*the rime-line is missing*)
1407 taught] *possibly* tau ght
1428 paſſion (*read* poiſon?)
1451 would (*read* I would?)
1457 they
1466 ſhoul'dſt
1468 neuer (*omit*?)
1478 heauy (*read* heaunly?)
1484 coul'dſt
1492 guliltles

1493 looke (*read* locke)
1504 her: Sould: you (*read* her? Sould: You?)
1506 Wie
1510 boue (*read* loue)
1525 *Bu*.] original *Bu*·
1526 caules (*read* cauſeles)
1542 founds
1543 didſt not (*read* dideſt?)
1560 Tis (*read* Thus?)
1566 your nuptiall (*read* our nuptiall?)
1589 heaue'n
1593 many (*read* man)
1601 You (*read* Your)
1604 he (*read* ſhe)
1654 *Sal*. doubt
1658 c.w. Youl'e] *so* B, C, Bodl., Dyce, Eton: Youlle A
1694 (*line too short*)
1781 anew,] *so* B, C, Bodl., Dyce, Eton: a new, A
1802 At (*read* As)
1844 power.) *Enter*
1849 I (*read* In?)
1855 ſecs (*read* ſays?)
1887 Gerarim (*read* Gerizim)
1905 ſcorniug] *turned* n *in original*
1938 Is (*read* In?)
1980 darke (*read* darken?)
1981 Our ſacred] *possibly* Ourſacred
1997 *Nun*. Go on, ſhe (*read* Go on. *Nun*. She?)
1999 cheefull
2002 (*line too short*)
2011 made her Lord, (*read* mad, her Lord)
2022 diuided, (*read* diuide,)
2050 ſhe (*read* he)
2090 faire,
2109 much a: (*read* much: a)
2124 li'ud.
2132 did (*read* died?)
2153, 2155 faine] *so* A. Bodl., Dyce: fame B, C, Eton
2177 voyd] *possibly* voy d

xi

LIST OF CHARACTERS

in order of appearance.

The extra leaf, found in the Huth copy, is said to contain a list of dramatis personae, but this is not now available.

MARIAM, wife to Herod.	ANTIPATER, her son.
ALEXANDRA, her mother.	ANANELL, the high priest.
SALOME, sister to Herod.	a Man of Silleus'.
SILLEUS, an Arabian.	SOHEMUS, guardian of Mariam in Herod's absence.
CONSTABARUS, husband to Salome.	
PHERORAS, brother to Herod.	HEROD, king of Judaea.
GRAPHINA, his love.	Nuntio.
two Sons of Babus.	a Butler.
DORIS, formerly wife to Herod, now repudiated.	a Soldier of Herod's.
	Chorus.

Attendants on Herod, guard.

The character described as 'Nuntio' in V. i, presumably also appears in IV. i, where the word is twice misprinted 'Nutio' (ll. 1262, 1263). The 'Butler' brings the drink in IV. iv: the name is conjectural since the text has nothing but the prefix 'Bu.' or 'Bu:' (ll. 1423, 1431, 1433, 1495, 1497, 1525). For the 'Soldier' see l. 1504. Herod's sister is called Salome or Salom according to the requirements of the metre.

No place is assigned for the scene; it is presumably in or before Herod's palace. The action is limited to one day.

With one exception the names of all the characters are taken from Josephus. He, however, does not name the slave-woman loved by Pheroras, who is here called Graphina. This name may, however, have been suggested by that of Glaphyra, the wife of a certain Alexander, mentioned in the same chapter as the incident of Pheroras' refusal of Herod's daughter. In Lodge's translation we actually find the marginal note: 'Herod greatly moued against Pheroras for affirming that he was in loue with Glaphyra', where 'he' properly refers to Herod though it might easily be taken to refer to Pheroras.

Note on the Source, Date, and Authorship of the Play.

Josephus gives two versions of the story of Mariam, one in the *Wars of the Jews*, the other in the *Antiquities*. Lady Cary uses the latter version. She follows Josephus fairly closely, but makes several alterations, sometimes compressing, sometimes amplifying, frequently transposing events, occasionally inventing scenes, to simplify the story and to observe the unities.

Many dramas have been based on this story, and most of these have been discussed by Landau: *Die Dramen von Herodes und Mariamne* (Zeitschrift für vergleichende Literaturgeschichte, ed. Koch, N.F. Bd. viii, ix. Weimar 1895–6). Before Lady Cary's drama appeared Dolce, Hans Sachs, and possibly Hardy had written their plays. Lady Cary does not seem to have used either the Italian, the German, or the French drama, but to have gone directly to Josephus for the subject-matter. It is true that Hardy's drama is to some extent similar to Lady Cary's work, whilst the dramas of Dolce and Hans Sachs contain much that is foreign to her play. Hardy's Pherore and Lady Cary's Pheroras do not appear in Dolce and Hans Sachs; in the argument of both dramas Hircanus is the father of Mariam: this mistake, however, is made once by Josephus, Lady Cary gives the correct relation throughout the drama, whilst Hardy does not do this. More striking is the similarity of Lady Cary l. 1983 ff. and Hardy v. 81 ff.: 'Que dis-je merité, mille morts plus cruelles', &c. But the similarities are not close enough to prove borrowing.

Before the appearance of Lady Cary's drama Latin, French, German, and English translations of Josephus had been published, and it is not quite clear whether Lady Cary used a Greek text or one of the translations. The following consideration points to the assumption that Lady Cary did not use a Greek text. In l. 1757 the name Asuerus occurs. In the Greek texts the name is Artaxerxes, but in some Latin texts there is a marginal gloss giving the name Assuerus, Asuerus. Thus the Latin text of 1514 (BM. 4515. f. 10) reads 'Cirus qui dictus est Artaxerxes in biblia est Assuerus', the Latin text of 1580 glosses 'Asuerus Rex Persarum'. A comparison of name-forms leads to no result. Lady Cary has Constabarus, Ananell, Babus sonnes, sonnes of Baba, Latin texts have Costobarus, Ananelus, Baba (gen. Babæ); Lodge has Costabarus Ananell (p. 386), Babas sonnes, &c. There are, however, good reasons for assuming that Lady Cary used Lodge's translation of Josephus (publ. 1602). Lodge translates *pincernam* 'butler', Lady Cary has a character Bu[tler]. Still more striking is the fact that Lady Cary combines the *pincerna* and *eunuchus* of the Latin texts (1580, p. 448), whilst in Lodge (p. 398) we read 'Mariammes most faithful servant' for 'eunuchum Mariammes fidissimum'. A slightly inattentive reader of Lodge might easily assume that the butler and the eunuch were one and the same person, as actually in the drama. There are, further, some verbal agreements: cp. Lady Cary, l. 1799 f.:

Am I the Mariam that presum'd so much &c.

and Lodge (p. 399): 'For being entertained by him, who intirely loued her ... she presumed vpon a great and intemperate libertie in her discourse'; Lady Cary's Argument 'and presently after by the instigation of Salome, she was beheaded', Lodge (p. 398) 'Mariamme by Salomes instigations is led to execution' (but the Latin gloss (p. 449) reads 'Mariamme Salomæ instinctu ad supplicium ducitur'); Lady Cary's Argument 'vnder colour of sport', Lodge (p. 386) 'pretending to duck him in sport'. Lodge's translation contains a preface 'To the courteous Reader'. Three passages resemble passages in Lady Cary: 'whereas they that sit in a plentifull banquet, in affecting all things, can make use of nothing', cp. Lady Cary, l. 180 ff.:

> But now he fared like a hungry guest,
> That to some plenteous festiuall is gone,
> Now this, now that, hee deems to eate were best,
> Such choice doth make him let them all alone.

Lodge: 'And truly in my opinion the chiefest ground of this difficulty [the reading of history aright], is the peruersness of our iudgements, which is the cause we the rather respect our own inclinations what they are, then the true life and force of example', cp. Lady Cary's Chorus to Act II. Lodge [By reading history we] 'sit and learne preuention by other mens perils, and grow amplie wise by forraine wreckes', cp. Lady Cary, ll. 2232–7.

If Lodge's translation was used the drama was probably written after 1602, although Lodge's work was licensed as early as 26 June, 1598 (Arber, iii. 119). The limits seem to be 1602 (Lodge's translation) and 23 March, 1604/5 (Philip Cary created knight).

There is some internal evidence for attributing the drama to Sir Henry Cary's (Viscount Falkland's) wife. After Lady Falkland's death a biography of her was written by one or more of her daughters and revised by one of her sons (*The Lady Falkland: her life*, &c., ed. R. S. 1861). The editor discusses the authorship of this biography in the introduction to his edition.

We know from this book that Lady Falkland was a great reader, that she herself wrote, and that she loved plays very much. There are some passages in the *Life* which are reflected in the drama. We read on p. 16 'she did always much disapprove the practice of satisfying oneself with their conscience being free from fault, not forbearing all that might have the least show or suspicion of uncomeliness or unfitness', and that she had 'Be and Seem' inscribed in her daughter's wedding ring. This maxim we find in the Chorus to Act III. Her letter to the king (p. 150) shows the attitude which Lady Falkland thought it right for a woman to adopt towards her husband. This is reflected in this chorus, and in ll. 1833-40, whilst the villain of the piece (Salome) holds quite opposite views. In the play we read (ll. 1795-6):

> My head waies downwards: therefore will I goe
> To try if I can sleepe away my woe.

On p. 17 of the *Life* we learn that Lady Falkland was frequently depressed, that she could sleep at will, and was in the habit of sleeping to cure depression. Less striking is a correspondence between p. 22 of the *Life*, where we are told that Lady Falkland would confess to 'finding much more delight in obliging than in being obliged', and ll. 657-8 of the play. Moreover, in the one work which is almost certainly by her, a translation of the *Reply of the Cardinal of Perron*, &c., 1630, she hid the identity of authorship. In this play the fact that copies are found without the leaf containing the sonnet possibly points to the supposition that Lady Cary wished to remain unknown to the general public.

Evidently Lady Falkland had written something to attract attention. In the translation of the *Reply* there are verses 'To the most noble Translatour', where we read:

> And though you know this where to weack a frame
> To rayse up higher the greatnesse of your name
> Which must from your owne rich inventions grow.

The publisher of Marston's *Works* 1633 dedicates them 'To the Right Honourable, the Lady Elizabeth Carey, Viscountess Falkland'. He does so 'because your Honour is well acquainted with the Muses'.

The dedication in John Davies's *Muses Sacrifice or Diuine Meditations* (London: printed by T. S. for George Norton, 1612) proves conclusively that Lady Falkland is the author of the play. This work is dedicated 'To the most noble, and no lesse deseruedly-renowned Ladyes, as well Darlings, as Patronesses, of the Muses; Lucy, Countesse of Bedford; Mary, Countesse-Dowager of Pembrooke; and Elizabeth,

Lady Cary, (Wife of S^r. Henry Cary:) Glories of Women'.
The last named he celebrates as follows:

> Cary (of whom Minerua stands in feare,
>   lest she, from her, should get Arts Regencie)
> Of Art so moues the great-all-mouing Spheare,
>   that eu'ry Orbe of Science moues thereby.
>
> Thou mak'st Melpomen proud, and my Heart great
>   of such a Pupill, who, in Buskin fine,
> With Feete of State, dost make thy Muse to mete
>   the Scenes of Syracuse and Palestine.
>
> Art, Language; yea; abstruse and holy Tongues,
>   thy Wit and Grace acquir'd thy Fame to raise;
> And still to fill thine owne, and others Songs;
>   thine, with thy Parts, and others, with thy praise.
>
> Such neruy Limbs of Art, and Straines of Wit
>   Times past ne'er knew the weaker Sexe to haue;
> And Times to come, will hardly credit it,
>   if thus thou giue thy Workes both Birth and Graue.

The works of these ladies remained unpublished apparently, for Davies, after remarking on the large amount of bad material printed, goes on to say:

> But your [*read* you] Three Graces, (whom our Muse would grace,
>   had she that glory, that our Philip had,
> That was the Beautie of Arts Soule and Face)
>   you presse the Presse with little you haue made.
>
> No; you well know the Presse so much is wrong'd,
>   by abiect Rimers that great Hearts doe scorne
> To haue their Measures with such Nombers throng'd,
>   as are so basely got, conceiu'd, and borne.

Many details concerning the Cary family are given in the *Herald and Genealogist*, edited by J. G. Nichols. From this work (vol. iii) the following facts are taken:

Extracts from Parish and other Registers.

Aldenham, Herts.

Baptisms.
1610. May 3. Miriall, ye dau. of ye right worshipfull Sir Philip Carye, knight. [This is the eldest child, or, at least, the earliest entry.]

Burials.
1623. Oct. 4. The Ladye Elizabeth, ye wife of the right wor^ll Sir Philippe Carye, knight.
1631. June 16. The right wor^ll Sir Philippe Cary.
1633. Sep. 25. The right hon^ble Henry, Lord Cary, Viscount Falkland.

Great Berkhampstead, Herts.

Marriages.
1586. Nov. 20. Jhon Savell, Esqr and Mrs Eliz^th Carye.

Registry of the Prerogative Court of Canterbury, Doctors' Commons, London:
(*Dorset* 33.) Sir Adolphe Carye, kt. Dat. March 16, 1604–5.
'... to my brother Sir Harry Cary, knt. ... to my brother Philip Carye ...' [the latter proved on 14 Apr. 1609 as Philip Cary, Knight.]
(*Fenner* 28.) Sir Wymond Carye, of Snettisham, co. Norfolk, knt. Dated Dec. 27, 1609.
'... to my nephew Sir Henry Cary, kt., son and heir app. of my brother Sir Edward Cary, kt. ... to my nephew Sir Philip Cary, kt., the youngest son of my said brother ...'

Henry Cary's eldest children were born at Burford (Oxfordshire). The registers here do not begin before 1612. According to Nichols (iii. 40) the eldest daughter, Catherine, was aged thirteen, and the eldest son, Lucius, was twelve, in 1622.

From the quotations from the wills it will be seen that Henry Cary was knighted before 16 March, 1604/5, but that his brother Philip was not. W. C. Metcalfe's *A Book of Knights*, London, 1885, contains the entries:

> Sr. Philip Cary, Herts. 23 March 1604[/5].
> Sr. Henry Cary, 3 Nov. 1616 [this is K.B.].
> Sr. Henry Cary, 12 July 1599 [at Dublin].

The Henry Cary who become a K.B. in 1616 is the later Viscount Falkland. The wills prove that he was already a knight at the time. It is not clear (and, as far as the drama is concerned, it is immaterial) when he was first knighted. He may possibly be the Henry Cary knighted at Dublin in 1599. The 'Sr. Philip Cary of Herts.', who was knighted [at Greenwich—see also W. A. Shaw, *The Knights of England*, London, 1906, ii. 137] in March 1604/5 is certainly his brother Philip. Philip is a rare name in the Cary family, whilst Henry is common.

The biography of Lady Falkland states:

'She was born in the year of our Lord 1585 or 1586, in Oxfordshire, at the priory of Burford, her father's house.' (p. 1.)

'At fifteen years old her father married her to one Sir Harry Carey (son to Sir Edward Carey, of Barkhamsteed in Herts), then master of the Jewel-house to Queen Elizabeth.' (p. 7.)

'She was married seven years without any child.' (p. 11.)

'She ... died ... the — day of October, the year of our Lord 1639, being three or four-and-fifty years old.' (p. 122.)

The name of Philip Cary's wife is given in the *Visitations of Hertfordshire 1572 and 1634* (Harleian MSS. 6147 and 1546), 1886, p. 136: 'Sir Philip Carey of Aldenham, co. Hertf. m. Elizabeth, da. of Richard Bland of co. York.'

THE TRAGEDIE OF MARIAM,
THE FAIRE Queene of Iewry.

Written by that learned, vertuous, and truly noble Ladie, E. C.

LONDON.
Printed by Thomas Creede, for Richard Hawkins, and are to be solde at his shoppe in Chancery Lane, neere vnto Sargeants Inne.
1613.

A 1 RECTO (B. M., C. 34. c. 9)

Actus primus.   Scœna prima.

Mariam sola.

HOw oft haue I with publike voyce runne on?
To censure *Romes* last *Hero* for deceit:
  Because he wept when *Pompey* life was gone,
Yet when he liu'd, hee thought his Name too great.
But now I doe recant, and *Roman* Lord,
Excuse too rash a judgement in a woman:
My Sexe pleads pardon, pardon then afford,
Mistaking is with vs, but too too common.
Now doe I finde by selfe Experience taught,
One Object yeelds both griefe and ioy:
You wept indeed, when on his worth you thought,
But ioyd that slaughter did your Foe destroy.
So at his death your Eyes true droppes did raine,
Whom dead, you did not wish aliue againe.
When *Herod* liu'd, that now is done to death,
Oft haue I wisht that I from him were free:
Oft haue I wisht that he might lose his breath,
Oft haue I wisht his Carkas dead to see.
Then Rage and Scorne had put my loue to flight,
That Loue which once on him was firmely set:
Hate hid his true affection from my sight,
And kept my heart from paying him his debt.
And blame me not, for *Herods* Iealousie
Had power euen constancie it selfe to change:
For hee by barring me from libertie,
To shunne my ranging, taught me first to range.
But yet too chast a Scholler was my hart,
To learne to loue another then my Lord:
To leaue his Loue, my lessons former part,

A 3

THE
TRAGEDIE
OF MARIAM,
THE FAIRE
Queene of Iewry.

Written by that learned,
vertuous, and truly noble Ladie,
E. C.

LONDON.
Printed by Thomas Creede, for Richard
Hawkins, and are to be folde at his shoppe
in Chancery Lane, neere vnto
Sargeants Inne.
1 6 1 3.

The Argument.

HErod the sonne of *Antipater* (an *Idumean,*) hauing crept by the fauor of the *Romanes,* into the Iewish Monarchie, married *Mariam* the daughrer of *Hircanus,* the rightfull *King and Priest,* and for her (besides her high blood, being of singular beautie) hee reputiated *Doris,* his former Wife, by whome hee had Children.

This *Mariam* had a Brother called *Aristobolus,* and next him and *Hircanus* his Graund-father, *Herod* in his Wiues right had the best title. Therefore to remooue them, he charged the first with treason: and put him to death; and drowned the second vnder colour of sport. *Alexandra,* Daughter to the one, and Mother to the other, accused him for their deaths before *Anthony.*

So when hee was forc'te to goe answere this Accusation at *Rome,* he left the custodie of his wife to *Iosephus* his Vncle, that had married his Sister *Salome,* and out of a violent affection (vnwilling any should enioy her after him) hee gaue strict and priuate commaundement, that if hee were slaine, shee should be put to death. But he returned with much honour, yet found his Wife extreamely discontented, to whom *Iosophus* had (meaning it for the best, to proue *Herod* loued her) reuealed his charge.

So by *Salomes* accusation hee put *Iosephus* to death, but was reconciled to *Mariam,* who still bare the death of her Friends exceeding hardly.

In this meane time *Herod* was againe necessarily to reuisite *Rome,* for *Cæsar* hauing ouerthrowne *Anthony* his

THE EPISTLE

great friend, was likely to make an alteration of his Fortune.

In his abfence, newes came to *Ierufalem* that *Cæfar* had put him to death, their willingnes it fhould be fo, together with the likelyhood, gaue this Rumor fo good credit, as *Sohemus* that had fuceeded *Iofephus* charge, fucceeded him likewife in reuealing it. So at *Herods* returne which was fpeedy and vnexpected, he found *Mariam* fo farre from ioye, that fhe fhewed apparant fignes of forrow. Hee ftill defiring to winne her to a better humour, fhe being very vnable to conceale her paffion, fell to vpbraiding him with her Brothers death. As they were thus debating, came in a fellow with a Cuppe of Wine, who hired by *Salome*, faide firft, it was a Loue potion, which *Mariam* defired to deliuer to the King: but afterwards he affirmed that it was a poyfon, and that *Sohemus* had tolde her fomewhat, which procured the vehement hate in her.

The King hearing this, more moued with Iealoufie of *Sohemus*, then with this intent of poyfon, fent her away, and prefently after by the inftigation of *Salome*, fhe was beheaded. Which rafhnes was afterward punifhed in him, with an intollerable and almoft Frantike paffion for her death.

Actus

Actus primus.   Scœna prima.

Mariam sola.

HOw oft haue I with publike voyce runne on?
To censure *Romes* last *Hero* for deceit:
Because he wept when *Pompeis* life was gone,
Yet when he liu'd, hee thought his Name too great.
But now I doe recant, and *Roman* Lord
Excuse too rash a judgement in a woman:
My Sexe pleads pardon, pardon then afford,
Mistaking is with vs, but too too common.
Now doe I finde by selfe Experience taught,
One Object yeelds both griefe and ioy:
You wept indeed, when on his worth you thought,
But ioyd that slaughter did your Foe destroy.
So at his death your Eyes true droppes did raine,
Whom dead, you did not wish aliue againe.
When *Herod* liu'd, that now is done to death,
Oft haue I wisht that I from him were free:
Oft haue I wisht that he might lose his breath,
Oft haue I wisht his Carkas dead to see.
Then Rage and Scorne had put my loue to flight,
That Loue which once on him was firmely set:
Hate hid his true affection from my sight,
And kept my heart from paying him his debt.
And blame me not, for *Herods* Iealousie
Had power euen constancie it selfe to change:
For hee by barring me from libertie,
To shunne my ranging, taught me first to range.
But yet too chast a Scholler was my hart,
To learne to loue another then my Lord:
To leaue his Loue, my lessons former part,

THE TRAGEDIE

I quickly learn'd, the other I abhord.
But now his death to memorie doth call,
The tender loue, that he to *Mariam* bare:
And mine to him, this makes thofe riuers fall,
Which by an other thought vnmoiftned are.
For *Ariftobolus* the lowlyeft youth
That euer did in Angels fhape appeare:
The cruell *Herod* was not mou'd to ruth,
Then why grieues *Mariam Herods* death to heare? 40
Why ioy I not the tongue no more fhall fpeake,
That yeelded forth my brothers lateft dome:
Both youth and beautie might thy furie breake,
And both in him did ill befit a Tombe.
And worthy Grandfire ill did he requite,
His high Affent alone by thee procur'd,
Except he murdred thee to free the fpright
Which ftill he thought on earth too long immur'd.
How happie was it that *Sohemus* maide
Was mou'd to pittie my diftreft eftate? 50
Might *Herods* life a truftie feruant finde,
My death to his had bene vnfeparate.   (beare,
Thefe thoughts haue power, his death to make me
Nay more, to wifh the newes may firmely hold:
Yet cannot this repulfe fome falling teare,
That will againft my will fome griefe vnfold.
And more I owe him for his loue to me,
The deepeft loue that euer yet was feene:
Yet had I rather much a milke-maide bee,
Then be the Monarke of *Iudeas* Queene. 60
It was for nought but loue, he wifht his end
Might to my death, but the vaunt-currier proue:
But I had rather ftill be foe then friend,
To him that faues for hate, and kills for loue.
Hard-hearted *Mariam*, at thy difcontent,
What flouds of teares haue drencht his manly face?
How canft thou then fo faintly now lament,
Thy trueft louers death, a deaths difgrace:
I now mine eyes you do begin to right

Th

OF MARIAM.

The wrongs of your admirer. And my Lord, 70
Long since you should haue put your smiles to flight,
Ill doth a widowed eye with ioy accord.
Why now me thinkes the loue I bare him then,
When virgin freedome left me vnrestraind:
Doth to my heart begin to creepe agen,
My passion now is far from being faind.
But teares flie backe, and hide you in your bankes,
You must not be to *Alexandra* seene:
For if my mone be spide, but little thankes
Shall *Mariam* haue, from that incensed Queene. 80

Actus primus: Scœna Secunda.

Mariam. Alexandra.

Alex: (mistake,
WHat meanes these teares? my *Mariam* doth
The newes we heard did tell the *Tyrants* end:
What weepst thou for thy brothers murthers sake,
Will euer wight a teare for *Herod* spend?
My curse pursue his breathles trunke and spirit,
Base *Edomite* the damned *Esaus* heire:
Must he ere *Iacobs* child the crowne inherit? 90
Must he vile wretch be set in *Dauids* chaire?
No *Dauids* soule within the bosome plac'te,
Of our forefather *Abram* was asham'd:
To see his seat with such a toade disgrac'te,
That seat that hath by *Iudas* race bene fain'd.
Thou fatall enemie to royall blood,
Did not the murther of my boy suffice,
To stop thy cruell mouth that gaping stood?
But must thou dim the milde *Hercanus* eyes?
My gratious father, whose too readie hand 100
Did lift this *Idumean* from the dust:
And he vngratefull catiffe did withstand,
The man that did in him most friendly trust.
What kingdomes right could cruell *Herod* claime,
Was he not *Esaus* Issue, heyre of hell?
Then what succession can he haue but shame?
Did not his Ancestor his birth-right sell?

O

THE TRAGEDIE

O yes, he doth from *Edoms* name deriue,
His cruell nature which with blood is fed:
That made him me of Sire and sonne depriue, 110
He euer thirsts for blood, and blood is red.
Weepst thou because his loue to thee was bent?
And readst thou loue in crimson caracters?
Slew he thy friends to worke thy hearts content?
No: hate may Iustly call that action hers.
He gaue the sacred Priesthood for thy sake,
To *Aristobolus.* Yet doomde him dead:
Before his backe the *Ephod* warme could make,
And ere the *Myter* setled on his head:
Oh had he giuen my boy no lesse then right, 120
The double oyle should to his forehead bring:
A double honour, shining doubly bright,
His birth annoynted him both Priest and King.
And say my father, and my sonne he slewe,
To royalize by right your Prince borne breath:
Was loue the cause, can *Mariam* deeme it true,
That *Mariam* gaue commandment for her death?
I know by fits, he shewd some signes of loue,
And yet not loue, but raging lunacie:
And this his hate to thee may iustly proue, 130
That sure he hates *Hercanus* familie.
Who knowes if he vnconstant wauering Lord,
His loue to *Doris* had renew'd againe?
And that he might his bed to her afford,
Perchance he wisht that *Mariam* might be slaine.

Nun: Doris, Alas her time of loue was past,
Those coales were rakte in embers long agoe:
If *Mariams* loue and she was now disgrast,
Nor did I glorie in her ouerthrowe.
He not a whit his first borne sonne esteem'd, 140
Because as well as his he was not mine:
My children onely for his owne he deem'd,
These boyes that did descend from royall line.
These did he stile his heyres to *Dauids* throne,
My *Alexander* if he liue, shall sit

In

OF MARIAM.

In the Maiefticke feat of *Salamon*,
To will it fo, did *Herod* thinke it fit.
   Alex. Why? who can claime from *Alexanders* brood
That Gold adorned Lyon-guarded Chaire?
Was *Alexander* not of *Dauids* blood?   150
And was not *Mariam Alexanders* heire?
What more then right could *Herod* then beftow,
And who will thinke except for more then right,
He did not raife them, for they were not low,
But borne to weare the Crowne in his defpight:
Then fend thofe teares away that are not fent
To thee by reafon, but by paffions power:
Thine eyes to cheere, thy cheekes to fmiles be bent,
And entertaine with ioy this happy houre.
Felicitie, if when fhee comes, fhe findes   160
A mourning habite, and a cheerleffe looke,
Will thinke fhe is not welcome to thy minde,
And fo perchance her lodging will not brooke.
Oh keepe her whileft thou haft her, if fhe goe
She will not eafily returne againe:
Full many a yeere haue I indur'd in woe,
Yet ftill haue fude her prefence to obtaine:
And did not I to her as prefents fend
A Table, that beft Art did beautifie
Of two, to whom Heauen did beft feature lend,   170
To woe her loue by winning *Anthony*:
For when a Princes fauour we doe craue,
We firft their Mynions loues do feeke to winne:
So I, that fought Felicitie to haue,
Did with her Mynion *Anthony* beginne,
With double flight I fought to captiuate
The warlike louer, but I did not right:
For if my gift had borne but halfe the rate,
The *Roman* had beene ouer-taken quite.
But now he fared like a hungry gueft,   180
That to fome plenteous feftiuall is gone,
Now this, now that, hee deems to eate were beft,
Such choice doth make him let them all alone.

THE TRAGEDIE

The boyes large forehead firſt did fayreſt ſeeme,
Then glaunſt his eye vpon my *Mariams* cheeke:
And that without compariſon did deeme,
VVhat was in eyther but he moſt did leeke.
And thus diſtracted, eythers beauties might
VVithin the others excellence was drown'd:
Too much delight did bare him from delight,   190
For eithers loue, the others did confound.
VVhere if thy portraiture had onely gone,
His life from *Herod, Anthony* had taken:
He would haue loued thee, and thee alone,
And left the browne *Egyptian* cleane forſaken.
And *Cleopatra* then to ſeeke had bene,
So firme a louer of her wayned face:
Then great *Anthonius* fall we had not ſeene,
By her that fled to haue him holde the chaſe.
Then *Mariam* in a *Romans* Chariot ſet,   200
In place of *Cleopatra* might haue ſhowne:
A mart of Beauties in her viſage met,
And part in this, that they were all her owne.
   Ma. Not to be Empriſe of aſpiring *Rome,*
Would *Mariam* like to *Cleopatra* liue:
With pureſt body will I preſſe my Toome,
And wiſh no fauours *Anthony* could giue.
   Alex. Let vs retire vs, that we may reſolue
How now to deale in this reuerſed ſtate:
Great are th'affaires that we muſt now reuolue,   210
And great affaires muſt not be taken late.

Actus primus.   Scœna tertia.

Mariam. Alexandra. Salome.

Salome.

MOre plotting yet? Why? now you haue the thing
For which ſo oft you ſpent your ſupliant breath:
   And *Mariam* hopes to haue another King,
Her eyes doe ſparkle ioy for *Herods* death.

Alex.

OF MARIAM.

Alex. If she desir'd another King to haue,
She might before she came in *Herods* bed
Haue had her wish. More Kings then one did craue,
For leaue to set a Crowne vpon her head.
I thinke with more then reason she laments,
That she is freed from such a sad annoy:
Who ist will weepe to part from discontent,
And if she ioy, she did not causelesse ioy.

Sal. You durst not thus haue giuen your tongue the raine,
If noble *Herod* still remain in life:
Your daughters betters farre I dare maintaine,
Might haue reioyc'd to be my brothers wife.

Mar. My betters farre, base woman t'is vntrue,
You scarce haue euer my superiors seene:
For *Mariams* seruants were as good as you,
Before she came to be *Iudeas* Queene.

Sal. Now stirs the tongue that is so quickly mou'd,
But more then once your collor haue I borne:
Your fumish words are sooner sayd then prou'd,
And *Salomes* reply is onely scorne.

Mar. Scorne those that are for thy companions held,
Though I thy brothers face had neuer seene,
My birth, thy baser birth so farre exceld,
I had to both of you the Princesse bene.
Thou party Iew, and party Edomite,
Thou Mongrell: issu'd from reiected race,
Thy Ancestors against the Heauens did fight,
And thou like them wilt heauenly birth disgrace.

Sal. Still twit you me with nothing but my birth,
What ods betwixt your ancestors and mine?
Both borne of *Adam*, both were made of Earth,
And both did come from holy *Abrahams* line.

Mar. I fauour thee when nothing else I say,
With thy blacke acts ile not pollute my breath:
Else to thy charge I might full iustly lay
A shamefull life, besides a husbands death.

Sal. Tis true indeed, I did the plots reueale,
That past betwixt your fauorites and you:
I ment not I, a traytor to conceale.

THE TRAGEDIE

Thus *Salome* your Mynion *Ioseph* flue.

Mar. Heauen, doſt thou meane this Infamy to ſmo-
Let ſlandred *Mariam* ope thy cloſed eare: (ther? 260
Selfe-guilt hath euer bene ſuſpitious mother,
And therefore I this ſpeech with patience beare.
No, had not *Salomes* vnſtedfaſt heart,
In *Ioſephus* ſtead her *Conſtabarus* plaſt,
To free her ſelfe, ſhe had not vſde the art,
To ſlander hapleſſe *Mariam* for vnchaſt.

Alex. Come *Mariam*, let vs goe: it is no boote
To let the head contend againſt the foote.

Actus primus. Scœna quarta.

Salome, Sola. 270

Liues *Salome*, to get ſo baſe a ſtile
As foote, to the proud *Mariam Herods* ſpirit:
In happy time for her endured exile,
For did he liue ſhe ſhould not miſſe her merit:
But he is dead: and though he were my Brother,
His death ſuch ſtore of Cinders cannot caſt
My Coales of loue to quench: for though they ſmo-
The flames a while, yet will they out at laſt. (ther
Oh bleſt *Arabia*, in beſt climate plaſt,
I by the Fruit will cenſure of the Tree: 280
Tis not in vaine, thy happy name thou haſt,
If all *Arabians* like *Silleus* bee:
Had not my Fate bene too too contrary,
When I on *Conſtabarus* firſt did gaze,
Silleus had beene obiect to mine eye:
Whoſe lookes and perſonage muſt allyes amaze.
But now ill Fated *Salome*, thy tongue
To *Conſtabarus* by it ſelfe is tide:
And now except I doe the Ebrew wrong
I cannot be the faire *Arabian* Bride: 290
What childiſh lets are theſe? Why ſtand I now
On honourable points? Tis long agoe

Since

OF MARIAM.

Since shame was written on my tainted brow:
And certaine tis, that shame is honours foe.
Had I vpon my reputation stood,
Had I affected an vnspotted life,
Iosephus vaines had still bene stuft with blood,
And I to him had liu'd a sober wife.
Then had I neuer cast an eye of loue,
On *Constabarus* now detested face,
Then had I kept my thoughts without remoue:
And blusht at motion of the least disgrace:
But shame is gone, and honour wipt away,
And Impudencie on my forehead sits:
She bids me worke my will without delay,
And for my will I will imploy my wits.
He loues, I loue; what then can be the cause,
Keepes me for being the *Arabians* wife?
It is the principles of *Moses* lawes,
For *Contabarus* still remaines in life,
If he to me did beare as Earnest hate,
As I to him, for him there were an ease,
A separating bill might free his fate:
From such a yoke that did so much displease.
Why should such priuiledge to man be giuen?
Or giuen to them, why bard from women then?
Are men then we in greater grace with Heauen?
Or cannot women hate as well as men?
Ile be the custome-breaker: and beginne
To shew my Sexe the way to freedomes doore,
And with an offring will I purge my sinne,
The lawe was made for none but who are poore.
If *Herod* had liu'd, I might to him accuse
My present Lord. But for the futures sake
Then would I tell the King he did refuse
The sonnes of *Baba* in his power to take.
But now I must diuorse him from my bed,
That my *Silleus* may possesse his roome:
Had I not begd his life he had bene dead,
I curse my tongue the hindrer of his doome,

THE TRAGEDIE

But then my wandring heart to him was fast,
Nor did I dreame of chaunge: *Silleus* said,
He would be here, and see he comes at last,
Had I not nam'd him longer had he staid.

Actus primus.   Scœna quinta.

Salome, Silleus.

Silleus. WEll found faire *Salome Iudæas* pride,
Hath thy innated wisedome found
To make *Silleus* deeme him deified,   (the way
By gaining thee a more then precious pray?   340
  Salo. I haue deuisde the best I can deuise,
A more imperfect meanes was neuer found:
But what cares *Salome*, it doth suffice
If our indeuours with their end be crown'd.
In this our land we haue an ancient vse,
Permitted first by our law-giuers head:
Who hates his wife, though for no iust abuse,
May with a bill diuorce her from his bed.
But in this custome women are not free,
Yet I for once will wrest it, blame not thou   350
The ill I doe, since what I do'es for thee,
Though others blame, *Silleus* should allow.
  Solleus. Thinkes *Salome, Silleus* hath a tongue
To censure her faire actions: let my blood
Bedash my proper brow, for such a wrong,
The being yours, can make euen vices good:
Arabia ioy, prepare thy earth with greene,
Thou neuer happie wert indeed till now:
Now shall thy ground be trod by beauties Queene,
Her foote is destin'd to depresse thy brow.   360
Thou shalt faire *Salome* commaund as much
As if the royall ornament were thine:
The weaknes of *Arabias* King is such,
The kingdome is not his so much as mine.
My mouth is our *Obodas* oracle,
Who thinkes not ought but what *Silleus* will?

And

And thou rare creature. *Asias* miracle,
Shalt be to me as It: *Obodas* ſtill.

Salome. Tis not for glory I thy loue accept,
Iudea yeelds me honours worthy ſtore: 370
Had not affection in my boſome crept,
My natiue country ſhould my life deplore.
Were not *Silleus* he with home I goe,
I would not change my *Palaſtine* for *Rome*:
Much leſſe would I a glorious ſtate to ſhew,
Goe far to purchaſe an *Arabian* toome.

Silleus. Far be it from *Silleus* ſo to thinke,
I know it is thy gratitude requites
The loue that is in me, and ſhall not ſhrinke
Till death doe ſeuer me from earths delights. (talke, 380

Salom. But whiſt; me thinkes the wolfe is in our (moſt?
Be gone *Silleus*, who doth here arriue?
Tis *Conſtabarus* that doth hither walke,
Ile find a quarrell, him from me to driue.

Sille. Farewell, but were it not for thy commaund,
In his deſpight *Silleus* here would ſtand.

Actus primus: Sœna Sexta.

Salome: Conſtabarus.

Conſt: OH *Salome*, how much you wrõg your name,
Your race, your country, and your husband 390
A ſtraungers priuate conference is ſhame,
I bluſh for you, that haue your bluſhing loſt.
Oft haue I found, and found you to my griefe,
Conſorted with this baſe *Arabian* heere:
Heauen knowes that you haue bin my comfort chiefe,
Then doe not now my greater plague appeare.
Now by the ſtately Carued edifice
That on Mount *Sion* makes ſo faire a ſhow,
And by the Altar fit for ſacrifice,
I loue thee more then thou thy ſelfe doeſt know. 400
Oft with a ſilent ſorrow haue I heard
How ill *Iudeas* mouth doth cenſure thee:

And

THE TRAGEDIE

And did I not thine honour much regard,
Thou shouldst not be exhorted thus for mee.
Didst thou but know the worth of honest fame,
How much a vertuous woman is esteem'd,
Thou wouldest like hell eschew deserued shame,
And seeke to be both chast and chastly deem'd.
Our wisest Prince did say, and true he said,
A vertuous woman crownes her husbands head. 410

Salome. Did I for this, vpreare thy lowe estate?
Did I for this requitall begge thy life,
That thou hadst forfeited haples fate?
To be to such a thankles wretch the wife.
This hand of mine hath lifted vp thy head,
Which many a day agoe had falne full lowe,
Because the sonnes of *Baba* are not dead,
To me thou doest both life and fortune owe.

Const. You haue my patience often exercisde,
Vse make my choller keepe within the bankes: 420
Yet boast no more, but be by me aduisde.
A benefit vpbraided, forfeits thankes:
I prethy *Salome* dismisse this mood,
Thou doest not know how ill it fits thy place:
My words were all intended for thy good,
To raise thine honour and to stop disgrace.

Sa. To stop disgrace? take thou no care for mee,
Nay do thy worst, thy worst I set not by:
No shame of mine is like to light on thee,
Thy loue and admonitions I defie. 430
Thou shalt no hower longer call me wife,
Thy Iealousie procures my hate so deepe:
That I from thee doe meane to free my life,
By a diuorcing bill before I sleepe.

Const. Are Hebrew women now trãsform'd to men?
Why do you not as well our battels fight,
And weare our armour? suffer this, and then
Let all the world be topsie turued quite.
Let fishes graze, beastes, swine, and birds descend,
Let fire burne downewards whilst the earth aspires: 440

Let

OF MARIAM.

Let Winters heat and Summers cold offend,
Let Thiſtels growe on Vines, and Grapes on Briers,
Set vs to Spinne or Sowe, or at the beſt
Make vs Wood-hewers, Waters-bearing wights:
For ſacred ſeruice let vs take no reſt,
Vſe vs as *Joſhua* did the *Gibonites*.

  Salom. Hold on your talke, till it be time to end,
For me I am reſolu'd it ſhall be ſo:
Though I be firſt that to this courſe do bend,
I ſhall not be the laſt full well I know.   450

  Conſt. Why then be witneſſe Heau'n, the Iudge of
Be witneſſe Spirits that eſchew the darke: (ſinnes,
Be witneſſe Angels, witneſſe Cherubins,
Whoſe ſemblance fits vpon the holy Arke:
Be witneſſe earth, be witneſſe *Paleſtine*,
Be witneſſe *Dauids* Citie, if my heart
Did euer merit ſuch an act of thine:
Or if the fault be mine that makes vs part,
Since mildeſt *Moſes* friend vnto the Lord,
Did worke his wonders in the land of *Ham*,   460
And flew the firſt-borne Babes without a ſword,
In ſigne whereof we eate the holy Lambe:
Till now that foureteene hundred yeeres are paſt,
Since firſt the Law with vs hath beene in force:
You are the firſt, and will I hope, be laſt,
That euer ſought her husband to diuorce.

  Salom. I meane not to be led by preſident,
My will ſhall be to me in ſtead of Law.

  Conſt. I feare me much you will too late repent,
That you haue euer liu'd ſo void of awe: 470
This is *Silleus* loue that makes you thus
Reuerſe all order: you muſt next be his.
But if my thoughts aright the cauſe diſcuſſe,
In winning you, he gaines no laſting bliſſe,
I was *Silleus*, and not long agoe
Joſephus then was *Conſtabarus* now:
When you became my friend you prou'd his foe,
As now for him you breake to me your vowd.

               C   *Salom.*

THE TRAGEDIE

Sal. If once I lou'd you, greater is your debt:
For certaine tis that you deserued it not.   480
And vndeserued loue we soone forget,
And therefore that to me can be no blot.
But now fare ill my once beloued Lord,
Yet neuer more belou'd then now abhord.

Const. Yet *Constabarus* biddeth thee farewell.
Farewell light creature. Heauen forgiue thy sinne:
My prophecying spirit doth foretell
Thy wauering thoughts doe yet but new beginne.
Yet I haue better scap'd then *Ioseph* did,
But if our *Herods* death had bene delayd,   490
The valiant youths that I so long haue hid,
Had bene by her, and I for them betrayd.
Therefore in happy houre did *Cæsar* giue
The fatall blow to wanton *Anthony*:
For had he liued, our *Herod* then should liue,
But great *Anthonius* death made *Herod* dye.
Had he enioyed his breath, not I alone
Had beene in danger of a deadly fall:
But *Mariam* had the way of perill gone,
Though by the Tyrant most belou'd of all.   500
The sweet fac'd *Mariam* as free from guilt
As Heauen from spots, yet had her Lord come backe
Her purest blood had bene vniustly spilt.
And *Salome* it was would worke her wracke.
Though all *Iudea* yeeld her innocent,
She often hath bene neere to punishment.

Chorus.

THose mindes that wholy dote vpon delight,
Except they onely ioy in inward good:
Still hope at last to hop vpon the right,   510
And so from Sand they leape in loathsome mud.
Fond wretches, seeking what they cannot finde,
For no content attends a wauering minde.
If wealth they doe desire, and wealth attaine,

Then

Then wondrous faine would they to honor lep:
Of meane degree they doe in honor gaine,
They would but wiſh a little higher ſtep.
   Thus ſtep to ſtep, and wealth to wealth they ad,
   Yet cannot all their plenty make them glad.

Yet oft we ſee that ſome in humble ſtate,
Are chreefull, pleaſant, happy, and content:
When thoſe indeed that are of higher ſtate,
With vaine additions do their thoughts torment.
   Th'one would to his minde his fortune binde,
   T'hother to his fortune frames his minde.

To wiſh varietie is ſigne of griefe,
For if you like your ſtate as now it is,
Why ſhould an alteration bring reliefe?
Nay change would then be fear'd as loſſe of blis.
   That man is onely happy in his Fate,
   That is delighted in a ſetled ſtate.

Still *Mariam* wiſht ſhe from her Lord were free,
For expectation of varietie:
Yet now ſhe ſees her wiſhes proſperous bee,
She grieues, becauſe her Lord ſo ſoone did die.
   Who can thoſe vaſt imaginations feede,
   Where in a propertie, contempt doth breede?

Were *Herod* now perchance to liue againe,
She would againe as much be grieued at that:
All that ſhe may, ſhe euer doth diſdaine,
Her wiſhes guide her to ſhe knowes not what.
   And ſad muſt be their lookes, their honor ſower,
   That care for nothing being in their power.

Actus ſecundus. Scœna prima.

Pheroras and Graphina.

Pher. 'TIs true *Graphina*, now the time drawes nye
    Wherin the holy Prieſt with hallowed right,

THE TRAGEDIE

The happy long defired knot fhall tie,
Pheroras and *Graphina* to vnite:
How oft haue I with lifted hands implor'd 550
This bleffed houre, till now implord in vaine,
Which hath my wifhed libertie reftor'd,
And made my fubiect felfe my owne againe.
Thy loue faire Mayd vpon mine eye doth fit,
Whofe nature hot doth dry the moyfture all,
Which were in nature, and in reafon fit
For my monachall Brothers death to fall:
Had *Herod* liu'd, he would haue pluckt my hand
From faire *Graphinas* Palme perforce: and tide
The fame in hatefull and defpifed band, 560
For I had had a Baby to my Bride:
Scarce can her Infant tongue with eafie voice
Her name diftinguifh to anothers eare:
Yet had he liu'd, his power, and not my choife
Had made me folembly the contract fweare.
Haue I not caufe in fuch a change to ioy?
What? though fhe be my Neece, a Princeffe borne:
Neere bloods without refpect: high birth a toy.
Since Loue can teach blood and kindreds fcorne.
What booted it that he did raife my head, 570
To be his Realmes Copartner, Kingdomes mate,
Withall, he kept *Graphina* from my bed,
More wifht by me then thrice *Iudeas* ftate.
Oh, could not he be skilfull Iudge in loue,
That doted fo vpon his *Mariams* face?
He, for his paffion, *Doris* did remoue.
I needed not a lawfull Wife difplace,
It could not be but he had power to iudge,
But he that neuer grudg'd a Kingdomes fhare,
This well knowne happineffe to me did grudge: 580
And ment to be therein without compare.
Elfe had I bene his equall in loues hoaft,
For though the Diadem on *Mariams* head
Corrupt the vulgar iudgements, I will boaft
Graphinas brow's as white, her cheekes as red.

Why

Why speaks thou not faire creature? moue thy tongue,
For Silence is a signe of discontent:
It were to both our loues too great a wrong
If now this hower do find thee sadly bent.
 Graph. Mistake me not my Lord, too oft haue I   590
Desir'd this time to come with winged feete,
To be inwrapt with griefe when tis too nie,
You know my wishes euer yours did meete:
If I be silent, tis no more but feare
That I should say too little when I speake:
But since you will my imperfections beare,
In spight of doubt I will my silence breake:
Yet might amazement tie my mouing tongue,
But that I know before *Pheroras* minde,
I haue admired your affection long: 600
And cannot yet therein a reason finde.
Your hand hath lifted me from lowest state,
To highest eminencie wondrous grace,
And me your hand-maid haue you made your mate,
Though all but you alone doe count me base.
You haue preserued me pure at my request,
Though you so weake a vassaile might constraine
To yeeld to your high will, then last not best
In my respect a Princesse you disdaine,
Then need not all these fauours studie craue,   610
To be requited by a simple maide:
And studie still you know must silence haue,
Then be my cause for silence iustly waide,
But studie cannot boote nor I requite,
Except your lowly hand-maides steadfast loue
And fast obedience may your mind delight,
I will not promise more then I can proue.
 Phero. That studie needs not let *Graphina* smile,
And I desire no greater recompence:
I cannot vaunt me in a glorious stile,   620
Nor shew my loue in far-fetcht eloquence:
But this beleeue me, neuer *Herods* heart
Hath held his Prince-borne beautie famed wife

In neerer place then thou faire virgin art,
To him that holds the glory of his life.
Should *Herods* body leaue the Sepulcher,
An d entertaine the feuer'd ghoft againe:
He fhould not be my nuptiall hinderer,
Except he hindred it with dying paine.
Come faire *Graphina*, let vs goe in ftate,
This wifh-indeered time to celebrate.

Actus 2.   Sœna. 2.

Conftabarus and *Babus Sonnes.*

Babus. 1. Sonne.

NOw valiant friend you haue our liues redeem'd,
Which liues as fau'd by you, to you are due:
Command and you fhall fee your felfe efteem'd,
Our liues and liberties belong to you.
This twice fixe yeares with hazard of your life,
You haue conceal'd vs from the tyrants fword:
Though cruell *Herods* fifter were your wife,
You durft in fcorne of feare this grace afford.
In recompence we know not what to fay,
A poore reward were thankes for fuch a merit,
Our trueft friendfhip at your feete we lay,
The beft requitall to a noble fpirit.   (youth,
  Conft. Oh how you wrong our friendfhip valiant
With friends there is not fuch a word as det:
Where amitie is tide with bond of truth,
All benefits are there in common fet.
Then is the golden age with them renew'd,
All names of properties are banifht quite:
Diuifion, and diftinction, are efchew'd:
Each hath to what belongs to others right.
And tis not fure fo full a benefit,
Freely to giue, as freely to require:
A bountious act hath glory following it,
They caufe the glory that the act defire.

All

OF MARIAM.

All friendſhip ſhould the patterne imitate,
Of *Ieſſes* Sonne and valiant *Ionathan*: 660
For neither Soueraignes nor fathers hate,
A friendſhip fixt on vertue feuer can.
Too much of this, tis written in the heart,
And need no amplifying with the tongue:
Now may you from your liuing tombe depart,
Where *Herods* life hath kept you ouer long.
Too great an iniury to a noble minde,
To be quicke buried, you had purchaſt fame,
Some yeares a goe, but that you were confinde.
While thouſand meaner did aduance their name. 670
Your beſt of life the prime of all your yeares,
Your time of action is from you bereft.
Twelue winters haue you operpaſt in feares:
Yet if you vſe it well, enough is left.
And who can doubt but you will vſe it well?
The ſonnes of *Babus* haue it by deſcent:
In all their thoughts each action to excell,
Boldly to act, and wiſely to inuent.
              Babus 2. *Sonne.*
Had it not like the hatefull cuckoe beene, 680
Whoſe riper age his infant nurſe doth kill:
So long we had not kept our ſelues vnſeene,
But *Conſtabarus* ſafely croſt our will:
For had the Tyrant fixt his cruell eye,
On our concealed faces wrath had ſwaide
His Iuſtice ſo, that he had forſt vs die.
And dearer price then life we ſhould haue paid,
For you our trueſt friend had falne with vs:
And we much like a houſe on pillers ſet,
Had cleane depreſt our prop, and therefore thus 690
Our readie will with our concealement met.
But now that you faire Lord are daungerleſſe,
The Sonnes of *Baba* ſhall their rigor ſhow:
And proue it was not baſenes did oppreſſe
Our hearts ſo long, but honour kept them low.
  Ba. 1. *Sonne.* Yet do I feare this tale of *Herods* death,
At laſt will proue a very tale indeed:

It

THE TRAGEDIE

It giues me ftrongly in my minde, his breath
Will be preferu'd to make a number bleed:
I wifh not therefore to be fet at large, 700
Yet perill to my felfe I do not leare:
Let vs for fome daies longer be your charge,
Till we of *Herods* ftate the truth do heare.

   Conft. What art thou turn'd a coward noble youth,
That thou beginft to doubt, vndoubted truth?

   Babus. 1. *Son.* Were it my brothers tongue that caft
I frõ his hart would haue the queftion out: (this doubt,
With this keene fauchion, but tis you my Lord
Againft whofe head I muft not lift a fword:
I am fo tide in gratitude *Conft.* belieue 710
You haue no caufe to take it ill,
If any word of mine your heart did grieue
The word difcented from the fpeakers will,
I know it was not feare the doubt begun,
But rather valour and your care of me,
A coward could not be your fathers fonne,
Yet know I doubts vnneceffarie be:
For who can thinke that in *Anthonius* fall,
Herod his bofome friend fhould fcape vnbrufde:
Then *Cæfar* we might thee an idiot call, 720
If thou by him fhould'ft be fo farre abufde.

   Babus. 2. *Sonne.* Lord *Conftab:* let me tell you this,
Vpon fubmiffion *Cæfar* will forgiue:
And therefore though the tyrant did amiffe,
It may fall out that he will let him liue.
Not many yeares agone it is fince I
Directed thither by my fathers care,
In famous *Rome* for twice twelue monthes did liue,
My life from *Hebrewes* crueltie to fpare,
There though I were but yet of boyifh age, 730
I bent mine eye to marke, mine eares to heare.
Where I did fee *Octauious* then a page,
When firft he did to *Iulions* fight appeare:
Me thought I faw fuch mildnes in his face,
And fuch a fweetnes in his lookes did grow,

Withall

Withall, commixt with so maiesticke grace,
His Phismony his Fortune did foreshow:
For this I am indebted to mine eye,
But then mine eare receiu'd more euidence,
By that I knew his loue to clemency,   740
How he with hottest choller could dispence.
  Const. But we haue more then barely heard the news,
It hath bin twice confirm'd. And though some tongue
Might be so false, with false report t'abuse,
A false report hath neuer lasted long.
But be it so that *Herod* haue his life,
Concealement would not then a whit auaile:
For certaine t'is, that she that was my wife,
Would not to set her accusation faile.
And therefore now as good the venture giue,   750
And free our selues from blot of cowardise:
As show a pittifull desire to liue,
For, who can pittie but they must despise?
            Babus first sonne.
I yeeld, but to necessitie I yeeld,
I dare vpon this doubt ingage mine arme:
That *Herod* shall againe this kingdome weeld,
And proue his death to be a false alarme.
           Babus second sonne.
I doubt it too: God grant it be an error,   760
Tis best without a cause to be in terror:
And rather had I, though my soule be mine,
My soule should lie, then proue a true diuine.
  Const. Come, come, let feare goe seeke a dastards
Vndanted courage lies in a noble brest.   (nest,

Actus 2.   Scœna 3.

Doris and Antipater.

Dor. YOur royall buildings bow your loftie side,
    And scope to her that is by right your Queen:

Let your humilitie vpbraid the pride 770
Of those in whom no due respect is seene:
Nine times haue we with Trumpets haughtie sound,
And banishing sow'r Leauen from our taste:
Obseru'd the feast that takes the fruit from ground.
Since I faire Citie did behold thee last,
So long it is since *Mariams* purer cheeke
Did rob from mine the glory. And so long
Since I returnd my natiue Towne to seeke:
And with me nothing but the sence of wrong.
And thee my Boy, whose birth though great it were, 780
Yet haue thy after fortunes prou'd but poore:
When thou wert borne how little did I feare
Thou shouldst be thrust from forth thy Fathers doore.
Art thou not *Herods* right begotten Sonne?
VVas not the haples *Doris, Herods* wife?
Yes: ere he had the Hebrew kingdome wonne,
I was companion to his priuate life.
VVas I not faire enough to be a Queene?
Why ere thou wert to me false Monarch tide,
My lake of beauty might as well be seene, 790
As after I had liu'd fiue yeeres thy Bride.
Yet then thine oath came powring like the raine,
Which all affirm'd my face without compare:
And that if thou might'st *Doris* loue obtaine,
For all the world besides thou didst not care.
Then was I yong, and rich, and nobly borne,
And therefore worthy to be *Herods* mate:
Yet thou vngratefull cast me off with scorne,
When Heauens purpose rais'd your meaner fate.
Oft haue I begd for vengeance for this fact, 800
And with deiected knees, aspiring hands
Haue prayd the highest power to inact
The fall of her that on my Trophee stands.
Reuenge I haue according to my will,
Yet where I wisht this vengeance did not light:
I wisht it should high-hearted *Mariam* kill.
But it against my whilome Lord did fight

With

OF MARIAM.

With thee sweet Boy I came, and came to try
If thou before his bastards might be plac'd
In *Herods* royall seat and dignitie. 810
But *Mariams* infants here are onely grac'd,
And now for vs there doth no hope remaine:
Yet we will not returne till *Herods* end
Be more confirmd, perchance he is not slaine.
So glorious Fortunes may my Boy attend,
For if he liue, hee'll thinke it doth suffice,
That he to *Doris* shows such crueltie:
For as he did my wretched life dispise,
So doe I know I shall despised die.
Let him but proue as naturall to thee, 820
As cruell to thy miserable mother:
His crueltie shall not vpbraided bee
But in thy fortunes. I his faults will smother.

Antipat. Each mouth within the Citie loudly cries
That *Herods* death is certaine: therefore wee
Had best some subtill hidden plot deuise,
That *Mariams* children might subuerted bee,
By poisons drinke, or else by murtherous Knife,
So we may be aduanc'd, it skils not how:
They are but Bastards, you were *Herods* wife, 830
And foule adultery blotteth *Mariams* brow.

Doris. They are too strong to be by vs remou'd,
Or else reuenges foulest spotted face:
By our detested wrongs might be approu'd,
But weakenesse must to greater power giue place.
But let vs now retire to grieue alone,
For solitarines best fitteth mone.

Actus secundus.   Scœna 4.

Silleus and Constabarus.

Silleus. WEll met *Iudean* Lord, the onely wight 840
 Silleus wisht to see. I am to call

Thy tongue to strict account. *Const.* For what despight
I ready am to heare, and answere all.
But if directly at the cause I gesse
That breeds this challenge, you must pardon me:
And now some other ground of fight professe,
For I haue vow'd, vowes must vnbroken be.
  Sill. What may be your expectation? let me know.
  Const. Why? ought concerning *Salom*, my sword
Shall not be welded for a cause so low, 850
A blow for her my arme will scorne t'afford.
  Sill. It is for slandering her vnspotted name,
And I will make thee in thy vowes despight,
Sucke vp the breath that did my Mistris blame,
And swallow it againe to doe her right.
  Const. I prethee giue some other quarrell ground
To finde beginning, raile against my name:
Or strike me first, or let some scarlet wound
Inflame my courage, giue me words of shame,
Doe thou our *Moses* sacred Lawes disgrace, 860
Depraue our nation, doe me some despight:
I'm apt enough to fight in any case,
But yet for *Salome* I will not fight.
  Sill. Nor I for ought but *Salome*: My sword
That owes his seruice to her sacred name:
Will not an edge for other cause afford,
In other fight I am not sure of fame.
  Const. For her, I pitty thee enough already,
For her, I therefore will not mangle thee:
A woman with a heart so most vnsteady, 870
Will of her selfe sufficient torture bee.
I cannot enuy for so light a gaine,
Her minde with such vnconstancie doth runne:
As with a word thou didst her loue obtaine,
So with a word she will from thee be wonne.
So light as her possessions for most day
Is her affections lost, to me tis knowne:
As good goe hold the winde as make her stay,
Shee neuer loues, but till she call her owne.

She

She meerly is a painted sepulcher, 880
That is both faire, and vilely foule at once:
Though on her out-side graces garnish her,
Her mind is fild with worse then rotten bones.
And euer readie lifted is her hand,
To aime destruction at a husbands throat:
For proofes, *Iosephus* and my selfe do stand,
Though once on both of vs, she seem'd to doat.
Her mouth though serpent-like it neuer hisses,
Yet like a Serpent, poysons where it kisses. (bite.
 Silleus. Well *Hebrew* well, thou bark'st, but wilt not 890
Const. I tell thee still for her I will not fight. (heart
 Sille: Why then I call thee coward. *Const:* From my
I giue thee thankes. A cowards hatefull name,
Cannot to valiant mindes a blot impart,
And therefore I with ioy receiue the same.
Thou know'st I am no coward: thou wert by
At the *Arabian* battaile th'other day:
And saw'st my sword with daring valiancy,
Amongst the faint *Arabians* cut my way.
The blood of foes no more could let it shine, 900
And twas inameled with some of thine.
But now haue at thee, not for *Salome*
I fight: but to discharge a cowards stile:
Here gins the fight that shall not parted be,
Before a soule or two indure exile. (my blood,
 Silleus. Thy sword hath made some windowes for
To shew a horred crimson phisnomie:
To breath for both of vs me thinkes twere good,
The day will giue vs time enough to die. (time,
 Const: With all my hart take breath, thou shalt haue 910
And if thou list a twelue month, let vs end:
Into thy cheekes there doth a palenes clime,
Thou canst not from my sword thy selfe defend.
What needest thou for *Salome* to fight, (her:
Thou hast her, and may'st keepe her, none striues for
I willingly to thee resigne my right,
For in my very soule I do abhorre her.

D 3

Thou

THE TRAGEDIE

Thou feeſt that I am freſh, vnwounded yet,
Then not for feare I do this offer make:
Thou art with loſſe of blood, to fight vnfit,   920
For here is one, and there another take.
   Silleus. I will not leaue, as long as breath remaines
Within my wounded body: ſpare your words,
My heart in bloods ſtead, courage entertaines,
Salomes loue no place for feare affords.
   Conſt: Oh could thy ſoule but propheſie like mine,
I would not wonder thou ſhould'ſt long to die:
For *Salome* if I aright diuine
Will be then death a greater miſerie.   (will,
   Sille: Then liſt, Ile breath no longer.   *Conſt:* Do thy 930
I hateles fight, and charitably kill. I, I, they fight,
Pittie thy ſelfe *Silleus*, let not death
Intru'd before his time into thy hart:
Alas it is too late to feare, his breath
Is from his body now about to part.
How far'ſt thou braue *Arabian*?   *Silleus* very well,
My legge is hurt, I can no longer fight:
It onely grieues me, that ſo ſoone I fell,
Before faire *Saloms* wrongs I came to right.   (feare,
   Conſt: Thy wounds are leſſe then mortall. Neuer   940
Thou ſhalt a ſafe and quicke recouerie finde:
Come, I will thee vnto my lodging beare,
I hate thy body, but I loue thy minde.
   Silleus. Thankes noble Iew, I ſee a courtious foe,
Sterne enmitie to friendſhip can no art:
Had not my heart and tongue engagde me ſo,
I would from thee no foe, but friend depart.
My heart to *Salome* is tide ſo faſt,
To leaue her loue for friendſhip, yet my skill
Shall be imploy'd to make your fauour laſt,   950
And I will honour *Conſtabarus* ſtill.
   Conſt: I ope my boſome to thee, and will take
Thee in, as friend, and grieue for thy complaint:
But if we doe not expedition make,
Thy loſſe of blood I feare will make thee faint.
                                            Chorus.

OF MARIAM.

Chorus.

TO heare a tale with eares preiudicate,
It spoiles the iudgement, and corrupts the sence:
That humane error giuen to euery state,
Is greater enemie to innocence. 960
    It makes vs foolish, heddy, rash, vniust,
    It makes vs neuer try before we trust.

It will confound the meaning, change the words,
For it our sence of hearing much deceiues:
Besides no time to Iudgement it affords,
To way the circumstance our eare receiues.
    The ground of accidents it neuer tries,
    But makes vs take for truth ten thousand lies.

Our eares and hearts are apt to hold for good,
That we our selues doe most desire to bee: 970
And then we drowne obiections in the flood
Of partialitie, tis that we see
    That makes false rumours long with credit past,
    Though they like rumours must conclude at last.

The greatest part of vs preiudicate,
With wishing *Herods* death do hold it true:
The being once deluded doth not bate,
The credit to a better likelihood due.
    Those few that wish it not the multitude,
    Doe carrie headlong, so they doubts conclude. 980

They not obiect the weake vncertaine ground,
Whereon they built this tale of *Herods* end:
Whereof the Author scarcely can be found,
And all because their wishes that way bend.
    They thinke not of the perill that ensu'th,
    If this should proue the contrary to truth.

THE TRAGEDIE

On this same doubt, on this so light a breath,
They pawne their liues, and fortunes. For they all
Behaue them as the newes of *Herods* death,
They did of most vndoubted credit call: 990
   But if their actions now doe rightly hit,
   Let them commend their fortune, not their wit.

Actus tertius: Scœna prima.

Pheroras: Salome.

Phero. VRge me no more *Graphina* to forsake,
    Not twelue howers since I married her
And doe you thinke a sisters power cane mak (for loue:
A resolute decree, so soone remoue?   (affects.
  Salome. Poore minds they are that honour not
Phero: Who hunts for honour, happines neglects. 1000
  Salom. You might haue bene both of felicitie,
And honour too in equall measure seasde.
  Phero: It is not you can tell so well as I,
What tis can make me happie, or displeasde.
  Salome. To match for neither beautie nor respects
One meane of birth, but yet of meaner minde,
A woman full of naturall defects,
I wonder what your eye in her could finde.   (wit,
  Phero: Mine eye found louelines, mine eare found
To please the one, and to enchant the other: 1010
Grace on her eye, mirth on her tongue doth sit,
In lookes a child, in wisedomes house a mother. (else,
  Salom: But say you thought her faire, as none thinks
Knowes not *Pheroras,* beautie is a blast:
Much like this flower which to day excels,
But longer then a day it will not last.   (show
  Phero: Her wit exceeds her beautie, *Salo:* Wit may
The way to ill, as well as good you know.
  Phero: But wisedome is the porter of her head,
And bares all wicked words from issuing thence. 1020
                                     Salome.

Sal. But of a porter, better were you sped,
If she against their entrance made defence.
   Phero. But wherefore comes the sacred *Ananell*,
That hitherward his hastie steppes doth bend?
Great sacrificer y'are arriued well,
Ill newes from holy mouth I not attend.

Actus tertius.   Scœna 2.

Pheroras. Salome. Ananell.

Ananell.

MY lippes, my sonne, with peacefull tidings blest,   1030
Shall vtter Honey to your listning eare:
A word of death comes not from Priestly brest,
I speake of life: in life there is no feare.
And for the newes I did the Heauens salute,
And fill'd the Temple with my thankfull voice:
For though that mourning may not me pollute,
At pleasing accidents I may reioyce.
   Pheror. Is *Herod* then reuiu'd from certaine death?
   Sall. What? can your news restore my brothers breath?
   Ana. Both so, and so, the King is safe and found,   1040
And did such grace in royall *Cæsar* meet:
That he with larger stile then euer crownd,
Within this houre Ierusalem will greet.
I did but come to tell you, and must backe
To make preparatiues for sacrifice:
I knew his death, your hearts like mine did racke,
Though to conceale it, prou'd you wise.
   Salom. How can my ioy sufficiently appeare?
   Phero. A heauier tale did neuer pierce mine eare.
   Salo. Now *Salome* of happinesse may boast.   1050
   Pheror. But now *Pheroras* is in danger most.
   Salom. I shall enioy the comfort of my life.
   Pheror. And I shall loose it, loosing of my wife.

THE TRAGEDIE

Salom. Ioy heart, for *Constan:* shall be slaine.
Phero. Grieue soule, *Graphina* shall from me be tane.
Salom. Smile cheekes, the faire *Silleus* shall be mine.
Phero. Weepe eyes, for I must with a child combine.
Salom. Well brother, cease your mones, on one con-
Ile vndertake to winne the Kings consent: (dition
Graphina still shall be in your tuition,
And her with you be nere the lesse content.
Phero. What's the condition? let me quickly know,
That I as quickly your command may act:
Were it to see what Hearbs in *Ophir* grow,
Or that the lofty *Tyrus* might be sackt.
Salom. Tis no so hard a taske: It is no more,
But tell the King that *Consta:* hid
The sonnes of *Baba*, done to death before:
And tis no more then *Consta.* did.
And tell him more that he for *Herods* sake,
Not able to endure his brothers foe:
Did with a bill our separation make,
Though loth from *Consta:* else to goe.
Phero. Beleeue this tale for told, Ile goe from hence,
In *Herods* eare the Hebrew to deface:
And I that neuer studied eloquence,
Doe meane with eloquence this tale to grace. *Exit.*
Salom. This will be *Constabarus* quicke dispatch,
Which from my mouth would lesser credit finde:
Yet shall he not decease without a match,
For *Mariam* shall not linger long behinde.
First Iealousie, if that auaile not, feare
Shalbe my minister to worke her end:
A common error moues not *Herods* eare,
Which doth so firmly to his *Mariam* bend.
She shall be charged with so horrid crime,
As *Herods* feare shall turne his loue to hate:
Ile make some sweare that she desires to clime,
And seekes to poyson him for his estate.
I scorne that she should liue my birth t'vpbraid,
To call me base and hungry Edomite:

With

OF MARIAM.

With patient show her choller I betrayd,
And watcht the time to be reueng'd by flite.
Now tongue of mine with scandall load her name,
Turne hers to fountaines, *Herods* eyes to flame:
Yet first I will begin *Pheroras* suite,
That he my earnest businesse may effect:
And I of *Mariam* will keepe me mute,
Till first some other doth her name detect.
Who's there, *Silleus* man? How fares your Lord?
That your aspects doe beare the badge of sorrow?

Silleus man.
He hath the marks of *Constabarus* sword,
And for a while desires your sight to borrow.

Salom. My heauy curse the hatefull sword pursue,
My heauier curse on the more hatefull arme
That wounded my *Silleus*. But renew
Your tale againe. Hath he no mortall harme?

Silleus man.
No signe of danger doth in him appeare,
Nor are his wounds in place of perill seene:
Hee bides you be assured you need not feare,
He hopes to make you yet *Arabias* Queene.

Salom. Commend my heart to be *Silleus* charge,
Tell him, my brothers suddaine comming now:
Will giue my foote no roome to walke at large,
But I will see him yet ere night I vow.

Actus 3.   Scœna 3.

Mariam and Sohemus.

Mariam.

SOhemus, tell me what the newes may be
That makes your eyes so full, your cheeks so blew?

Sohem. I know not how to call them. Ill for me
Tis sure they are: not so I hope for you.
Herod. *Mari.* Oh, what of *Herod*? *Sohem.* *Herod* liues.
How! liues? What in some Caue or forrest hid?

E 2   *Sohem.* Nay,

THE TRAGEDIE

Sohem. Nay, backe return'd with honor. *Cæsar* giues
Him greater grace then ere *Anthonius* did.
 Mari. Foretell the ruine of my family,
Tell me that I shall see our Citie burnd: 1130
Tell me I shall a death disgracefull die,
But tell me not that *Herod* is returnd.
 Sohem. Be not impatient Madam, be but milde,
His loue to you againe will soone be bred:
 Mar. I will not to his loue be reconcilde,
With solemne vowes I haue forsworne his Bed.
 Sohem. But you must breake those vowes.
 Mar. Ile rather breake
The heart of *Mariam.* Cursed is my Fate:
But speake no more to me, in vaine ye speake 1140
To liue with him I so profoundly hate.
 Sohem. Great Queene, you must to me your pardon
Sohemus cannot now your will obey: (giue,
If your command should me to silence driue,
It were not to obey, but to betray.
Reiect, and slight my speeches, mocke my faith,
Scorne my obseruance, call my counsell nought:
Though you regard not what *Sohemus* saith,
Yet will I euer freely speake my thought.
I feare ere long I shall faire *Mariam* see 1150
In wofull state, and by her selfe vndone:
Yet for your issues sake more temp'rate bee,
The heart by affabilitie is wonne.
 Mari. And must I to my Prison turne againe?
Oh, now I see I was an hypcorite:
I did this morning for his death complaine,
And yet doe mourne, becau se he liues ere night.
When I his death beleeu'd, compassion wrought,
And was the stickler twixt my heart and him:
But now that Curtaine's drawne from off my thought, 1160
Hate doth appeare againe with visage grim:
And paints the face of *Herod* in my heart,
In horred colours with detested looke:
Then feare would come, but scorne doth play her part,
And

OF MARIAM.

And faith that fcorne with feare can neuer brooke.
I know I could inchaine him with a fmile:
And lead him captiue with a gentle word,
I fcorne my looke fhould euer man beguile,
Or other fpeech, then meaning to afford.
Elfe *Salome* in vaine might fpend her winde,   1170
In vaine might *Herods* mother whet her tongue:
In vaine had they complotted and combinde,
For I could ouerthrow them all ere long.
Oh what a fhelter is mine innocence,
To fhield me from the pangs of inward griefe:
Gainft all mifhaps it is my faire defence,
And to my forrowes yeelds a large reliefe.
To be commandreffe of the triple earth,
And fit in fafetie from a fall fecure:
To haue all nations celebrate my birth,   1180
I would not that my fpirit were impure.
Let my diftreffed ftate vnpittied bee,
Mine innocence is hope enough for mee.   *Exit.*

   Sohem: Poore guiltles Queene. Oh that my wifh
A little temper now about thy heart: (might place
Vnbridled fpeech is *Mariams* worft difgrace,
And will indanger her without defart.
I am in greater hazard. O're my head,
The fattall axe doth hang vnftedily:
My difobedience once difcouered,   1190
Will fhake it downe: *Sohemus* fo fhall die.
For when the King fhall find, we thought his death
Had bene as certaine as we fee his life:
And markes withall I flighted fo his breath,
As to preferue aliue his matchles wife.
Nay more, to giue to *Alexanders* hand
The regall dignitie. The foueraigne power,
How I had yeelded vp at her command,
The ftrength of all the citie, *Dauids* Tower.
What more then common death may I expect,   1200
Since I too well do know his crueltie:
Twere death, a word of *Herods* to neglect,

E 3   What

What then to doe directly contrarie?
Yet life I quite thee with a willing spirit,
And thinke thou could'st not better be imploi'd:
I forfeit thee for her that more doth merit,
Ten such were better dead then she destroi'd.
But fare thee well chast Queene, well may I see
The darknes palpable, and riuers part:
The sunne stand still. Nay more retorted bee,
But neuer woman with so pure a heart.
Thine eyes graue maiestie keepes all in awe,
And cuts the winges of euery loose desire:
Thy brow is table to the modest lawe,
Yet though we dare not loue, we may admire.
And if I die, it shall my soule content,
My breath in *Mariams* seruice shall be spent.

Chorus.

Tis not enough for one that is a wife
  To keepe her spotles from an act of ill:
    But from suspition she should free her life,
And bare her selfe of power as well as will.
    Tis not so glorious for her to be free,
    As by her proper selfe restrain'd to bee.

When she hath spatious ground to walke vpon,
Why on the ridge should she desire to goe?
It is no glory to forbeare alone,
Those things that may her honour ouerthrowe.
    But tis thanke-worthy, if she will not take
    All lawfull liberties for honours sake.

That wife her hand against her fame doth reare,
That more then to her Lord alone will giue
A priuate word to any second eare,
And though she may with reputation liue.
    Yet though most chast, she doth her glory blot,
    And wounds her honour, though she killes it not.
        When

OF MARIAM.

When to their Husbands they themselues doe bind,
Doe they not wholy giue themselues away?
Or giue they but their body not their mind,
Reseruing that though best, for others pray?   1240
   No sure, their thoughts no more can be their owne,
   And therefore should to none but one be knowne.

Then she vsurpes vpon anothers right,
That seekes to be by publike language grac't:
And though her thoughts reflect with purest light,
Her mind if not peculiar is not chast.
   For in a wife it is no worse to finde,
   A common body, then a common minde.

And euery mind though free from thought of ill,
That out of glory seekes a worth to show: 1250
When any's eares but one therewith they fill,
Doth in a sort her purenes ouerthrow.
   Now *Mariam* had, (but that to this she bent)
   Beene free from feare, as well as innocent.

Actus quartus: Scœna prima.

Enter Herod and his attendants.
Herod.

HAile happie citie, happie in thy store,
   And happy that thy buildings such we see:
   More happie in the Temple where w'adore,   1260
But most of all that *Mariam* liues in thee.
Art thou return'd? how fares my *Mariam*? *Enter Nutio.*
   Nutio. She's well my Lord, and will anon be here
As you commanded. *Her:* Muffle vp thy browe
Thou daies darke taper. *Mariam* will appeare.
And where she shines, we need not thy dimme light,
Oh hast thy steps rare creature, speed thy pace:
And let thy presence make the day more bright,
And cheere the heart of *Herod* with thy face.

                                 It

THE TRAGEDIE

It is an age since I from *Mariam* went,   1270
Me thinkes our parting was in *Dauids* daies:
The houres are so increast by discontent,
Deepe sorrow, *Iosua*like the season staies:
But when I am with *Mariam*, time runnes on,
Her sight, can make months, minutes, daies of weekes:
An hower is then no sooner come then gon.
When in her face mine eye for wonders seekes.
You world commanding citie, *Europes* grace,
Twice hath my curious eye your streets suruai'd,
And I haue seene the statue filled place,   1280
That once if not for griefe had bene betrai'd.
I all your *Roman* beauties haue beheld,
And seene the showes your *Ediles* did prepare,
I saw the sum of what in you exceld,
Yet saw no miracle like *Mariam* rare.
The faire and famous *Liuia*, *Cæsars* loue,
The worlds commaunding Mistresse did I see:
Whose beauties both the world and *Rome* approue,
Yet *Mariam*: *Liuia* is not like to thee.
Be patient but a little, while mine eyes   1290
Within your compast limits be contain'd:
That obiect straight shall your desires suffice,
From which you were so long a while restrain'd.
How wisely *Mariam* doth the time delay,
Least suddaine ioy my sence should suffocate:
I am prepar'd, thou needst no longer stay:
Whose there, my *Mariam*, more then happie fate?
Oh no, it is *Pheroras*, welcome Brother,
Now for a while, I must my passion smother.

Actus quartus. Scœna secunda.   1300

Herod. Pheroras.

Pheroras.

ALl health and safetie waite vpon my Lord,
And may you long in prosperous fortunes liue

With

OF MARIAM.

With *Rome* commanding *Cæsar*; at accord,
And haue all honors that the world can giue.

   Herod. Oh brother, now thou speakst not from thy
No, thou hast strooke a blow at *Herods* loue: (hart,
That cannot quickly from my memory part,
Though *Salome* did me to pardon moue.   1310
Valiant *Phasaelus*, now to thee farewell,
Thou wert my kinde and honorable brother:
Oh haples houre, when you selfe striken fell,
Thou fathers Image, glory of thy mother.
Had I desir'd a greater sute of thee,
Then to withhold thee from a harlots bed,
Thou wouldst haue granted it: but now I see
All are not like that in a wombe are bred.
Thou wouldst not, hadst thou heard of *Herods* death,
Haue made his buriall time, thy bridall houre: 1320
Thou wouldst with clamours, not with ioyfull breath,
Haue show'd the newes to be not sweet but soure.

   Phero. *Phasaelus* great worth I know did staine
Pheroras petty valour: but they lie
(Excepting you your selfe) that dare maintaine,
That he did honor *Herod* more then I.
For what I showd, loues power constraind me show,
And pardon louing faults for *Mariams* sake.

   Herod. *Mariam*, where is she? *Phero.* Nay, I do not
But absent vse of her faire name I make: (know, 1330
You haue forgiuen greater faults then this,
For *Constabarus* that against you will
Preseru'd the sonnes of *Baba*, liues in blisse,
Though you commanded him the youths to kill.

   Herod. Goe, take a present order for his death,
And let those traytors feele the worst of feares:
Now *Salome* will whine to begge his breath,
But Ile be deafe to prayers: and blind to teares.

   Phero. He is my Lord from *Salom* diuorst,
Though her affection did to leaue him grieue: 1340
Yet was she by her loue to you inforst,
To leaue the man that would your foes relieue.

F   *Herod*

THE TRAGEDIE

Hero. Then haste them to their death. I will requite
Thee gentle *Mariam. Salom.* I meane
The thought of *Mariam* doth so steale my spirit,
My mouth from speech of her I cannot weane. *Exit.*

Actus 4.   Scœna 3.

Herod. Mariam.

Herod.

And heere she comes indeed: happily met   1350
My best, and deerest halfe: what ailes my deare?
  Thou doest the difference certainly forget
Twixt Duskey habits, and a time so cleare.
  Mar. My Lord, I suit my garment to my minde,
And there no cheerfull colours can I finde.
  Herod. Is this my welcome? haue I longd so much
To see my dearest *Mariam* discontent?
What ist that is the cause thy heart to touch?
Oh speake, that I thy sorrow may preuent.
Art thou not *Iuries* Queene, and *Herods* too?   1360
Be my Commandres, be my Soueraigne guide:
To be by thee directed I will woo,
For in thy pleasure lies my highest pride.
Or if thou thinke *Iudæas* narrow bound,
Too strict a limit for thy great command:
Thou shalt be Empresse of *Arabia* crownd,
For thou shalt rule, and I will winne the Land.
Ile robbe the holy *Dauids* Sepulcher
To giue thee wealth, if thou for wealth do care:
Thou shalt haue all, they did with him inter,   1370
And I for thee will make the Temple bare.
  Mar. I neither haue of power nor riches want,
I haue enough, nor doe I wish for more:
Your offers to my heart no ease can grant,
Except they could my brothers life restore.
No, had you wisht the wretched *Mariam* glad,

Or

Or had your loue to her bene truly tide:
Nay, had you not defir'd to make her fad,
My brother nor my Grandfyre had not dide.

Her. Wilt thou beleeue no oathes to cleere thy Lord? 1380
How oft haue I with execration fworne:
Thou art by me belou'd, by me ador'd,
Yet are my proteftations heard with fcorne.
Hercanus plotted to depriue my head
Of this long fetled honor that I weare:
And therefore I did iuftly doome him dead,
To rid the Realme from perill, me from feare.
Yet I for *Mariams* fake doe fo repent
The death of one: whofe blood fhe did inherit:
I wifh I had a Kingdomes treafure fpent, 1390
So I had nere expeld *Hercanus* fpirit.
As I affected that fame noble youth,
In lafting infamie my name inrole:
If I not mournd his death with heartie truth.
Did I not fhew to him my earneft loue,
When I to him the Priefthood did reftore?
And did for him a liuing Prieft remoue,
Which neuer had bene done but once before.

Mariam. I know that mou'd by importunitie,
You made him Prieft, and fhortly after die. 1400

Herod. I will not fpeake, vnles to be beleeu'd,
This froward humor will not doe you good:
It hath too much already *Herod* grieu'd,
To thinke that you on termes of hate haue ftood.
Yet fmile my deareft *Mariam*, doe but fmile,
And I will all vnkind conceits exile.

Mari. I cannot frame difguife, nor neuer taught
My face a looke diffenting from my thought.

Herod. By heau'n you vexe me, build not on my loue.

Mari. I wil not build on fo vnftable ground. 1410

Herod. Nought is fo fixt, but peeuifhnes may moue.

Mar. Tis better fleighteft caufe then none were foũd.

Herod. Be iudge your felfe, if euer *Herod* fought
Or would be mou'd a caufe of change to finde:

Yet

THE TRAGEDIE

Yet let your looke declare a milder thought,
My heart againe you shall to *Mariam* binde.
How oft did I for you my Mother chide,
Reuile my Sister, and my brother rate:
And tell them all my *Mariam* they belide,
Distrust me still, if these be signes of hate.   1420

Actus 4.   Scœna 4.

Herod.

WHat hast thou here?   *Bu.* A drinke procuring
The Queene desir'd me to deliuer it.   (loue,
   Mar. Did I: some hatefull practise this will proue,
Yet can it be no worse then Heauens permit.
   Herod. Confesse the truth thou wicked instrument,
To her outragious will, tis passion sure:
Tell true, and thou shalt scape the punishment,
Which if thou doe conceale thou shalt endure.   1430
   Bu. I know not, but I doubt it be no lesse,
Long since the hate of you her heart did cease.
   Herod. Know'st thou the cause thereof? *Bu.* My Lord
Sohemus told the tale that did displease.   (I gesse,
   Herod. Oh Heauen! *Sohemus* false! Goe let him die,
Stay not to suffer him to speake a word:
Oh damned villaine, did he falsifie
The oath he swore eu'n of his owne accord?
Now doe I know thy falshood, painted Diuill
Thou white Inchantres. Oh thou art so foule,   1440
That Ysop cannot clense thee worst of euill.
A beautious body hides a loathsome soule,
Your loue *Sohemus* mou'd by his affection,
Though he haue euer heretofore bene true:
Did blab forsooth, that I did giue direction,
If we were put to death to slaughter you.
And you in blacke reuenge attended now
To adde a murther to your breach of vow.
   Mar. Is this a dream? *Her.* Oh Heauen, that t'were no
Ile giue my Realme to who can proue it so: (more, 1450

I

OF MARIAM.

I would I were like any begger poore,
So I for falſe my *Mariam* did not know.
Foule pith contain'd in the faireſt rinde,
That euer grac'd a Cædar. Oh thine eye
Is pure as heauen, but impure thy minde,
And for impuritie ſhall *Mariam* die.
Why didſt thou loue *Sohemus*? *Mar:* they can tell
That ſay I lou'd him, *Mariam* ſaies not ſo.
    Herod. Oh cannot impudence the coales expell,
That for thy loue in *Herods* boſome glowe: 1460
It is as plaine as water, and deniall
Makes of thy falſehood but a greater triall.
Haſt thou beheld thy ſelfe, and couldſt thou ſtaine
So rare perfection: euen for loue of thee
I doe profoundly hate thee. Wert thou plaine,
Thou ſhoul'dſt the wonder of *Iudea* bee.
But oh thou art not. Hell it ſelfe lies hid
Beneath thy heauenly ſhow. Yet neuer wert thou chaſt:
Thou might'ſt exalt, pull downe, command, forbid,
And be aboue the wheele of fortune plaſt.   1470
Hadſt thou complotted *Herods* maſſacre,
That ſo thy ſonne a Monarch might be ſtilde,
Not halfe ſo grieuous ſuch an action were,
As once to thinke, that *Mariam* is defilde.
Bright workmanſhip of nature ſulli'd ore,
With pitched darknes now thine end ſhall bee:
Thou ſhalt not liue faire fiend to cozen more,
With heauy ſemblance, as thou couſnedſt mee.
Yet muſt I loue thee in deſpight of death,
And thou ſhalt die in the diſpight of loue: 1480
For neither ſhall my loue prolong thy breath,
Nor ſhall thy loſſe of breath my loue remoue.
I might haue ſeene thy falſehood in thy face,
Where coul'dſt thou get thy ſtares that ſeru'd for eyes?
Except by theft, and theft is foule diſgrace:
This had appear'd before were *Herod* wiſe,
But I'me a ſot, a very ſot, no better:
My wiſedome long agoe a wandring fell,

F 3   Thy

THE TRAGEDIE

Thy face incountring it, my wit did fetter,
And made me for delight my freedome fell. 1490
Giue me my heart falfe creature, tis a wrong,
My guliltles heart fhould now with thine be flaine:
Thou hadft no right to looke it vp fo long,
And with vfurpers name I *Mariam* ftaine.

Enter Bu:

He: Haue you defign'd *Sohemus* to his end? (guard
Bu: I haue my Lord. *Herod:* Then call our royall
To doe as much for *Mariam*, they offend
Leaue ill vnblam'd, or good without reward.
Here take her to her death. Come backe, come backe, 1500
What ment I to depriue the world of light:
To muffle *Iury* in the fouleft blacke,
That euer was an oppofite to white.
Why whither would you carrie her: *Sould:* you bad
We fhould conduct her to her death my Lord.

Hero: Wie fure I did not, *Herod* was not mad,
Why fhould fhe feele the furie of the fword?
Oh now the griefe returnes into my heart,
And pulles me peecemeale: loue and hate doe fight:
And now hath boue acquir'd the greater part, 1510
Yet now hath hate, affection conquer'd quite.
And therefore beare her hence: and *Hebrew* why
Seaze you with Lyons pawes the faireft lam
Of all the flocke? fhe muft not, fhall not, die,
Without her I moft miferable am.
And with her more then moft, away, away,
But beare her but to prifon not to death:
And is fhe gon indeed, ftay villaines ftay,
Her lookes alone preferu'd your Soueraignes breath.
Well let her goe, but yet fhe fhall not die, 1520
I cannot thinke fhe ment to poifon me:
But certaine tis fhe liu'd too wantonly,
And therefore fhall fhe neuer more be free.

Actus

Actus 4. Scœna 5.

Bu. Foule villaine, can thy pitchie coloured soule
Permit thine eare to heare her caules doome?
And not inforce thy tongue that tale controule,
That must vniustly bring her to her toome.
Oh *Salome* thou hast thy selfe repaid,
For all the benefits that thou hast done: 1530
Thou art the cause I haue the queene betraid,
Thou hast my hart to darkest false-hood wonne.
I am condemn'd, heau'n gaue me not my tongue
To slander innocents, to lie, deceiue:
To be the hatefull instrument to wrong,
The earth of greatest glory to bereaue.
My sinne ascends and doth to heau'n crie,
It is the blackest deed that euer was:
And there doth sit an Angell notarie,
That doth record it downe in leaues of brasse.   1540
Oh how my heart doth quake: *Achitophel,*
Thou founds a meanes thy selfe from shame to free:
And sure my soule approues thou didst not well,
All follow some, and I will follow thee.

Actus 4. Scœna 6.

Constabarus, Babus Sonnes, and their guard.

Const: Now here we step our last, the way to death,
We must not tread this way a second time:
Yet let vs resolutely yeeld our breath,
Death is the onely ladder, Heau'n to clime.   (resigne, 1550
   Babus 1. *Sonne.* With willing mind I could my selfe
But yet it grieues me with a griefe vntold:
Our death should be accompani'd with thine,
Our friendship we to thee haue dearely sold.

Const:

THE TRAGEDIE

Const. Still wilt thou wrong the sacred name of friend?
Then should'st thou neuer stile it friendship more:
But base mechanicke traffique that doth lend,
Yet will be sure they shall the debt restore.
I could with needlesse complement returne,
Tis for thy ceremonie I could say: 1560
Tis I that made the fire your house to burne,
For but for me she would not you betray.
Had not the damned woman sought mine end,
You had not bene the subiect of her hate:
You neuer did her hatefull minde offend,
Nor could your deaths haue freed your nuptiall fate.
Therefore faire friends, though you were still vnborne,
Some other subtiltie deuisde should bee:
Were by my life, though guiltles should be torne,
Thus haue I prou'd, tis you that die for mee. 1570
And therefore should I weakely now lament,
You haue but done your duties, friends should die:
Alone their friends disaster to preuent,
Though not compeld by strong necessitie.
But now farewell faire citie, neuer more
Shall I behold your beautie shining bright:
Farewell of *Iewish* men the worthy store,
But no farewell to any female wight.
You wauering crue: my curse to you I leaue,
You had but one to giue you any grace: 1580
And you your selues will *Mariams* life bereaue,
Your common-wealth doth innocencie chase.
You creatures made to be the humane curse,
You Tygers, Lyonesses, hungry Beares,
Teare massacring *Hienas*: nay far worse,
For they for pray doe shed their fained teares.
But you will weepe, (you creatures crosse to good)
For your vnquenched thirst of humane blood:
You were the Angels cast from heaue'n for pride,
And still doe keepe your Angels outward show, 1590
But none of you are inly beautifide,
For still your heau'n depriuing pride doth grow.

Did

OF MARIAM.

Did not the sinnes of many require a scourge,
Your place on earth had bene by this withstood:
But since a flood no more the world must purge,
You staid in office of a second flood.
You giddy creatures, sowers of debate,
You'll loue to day, and for no other cause,
But for you yesterday did deply hate,
You are the wreake of order, breach of lawes.   1600
You best, are foolish, froward, wanton, vaine,
Your worst adulterous, murderous, cunning, proud:
And *Salome* attends the latter traine,
Or rather he their leader is allowd.
I do the sottishnesse of men bewaile,
That doe with following you inhance your pride:
T'were better that the humane race should faile,
Then be by such a mischiefe multiplide.
Chams seruile curse to all your sexe was giuen,
Because in Paradise you did offend: 1610
Then doe we not resist the will of Heauen,
When on your willes like seruants we attend?
You are to nothing constant but to ill,
You are with nought but wickednesse indude:
Your loues are set on nothing but your will,
And thus my censure I of you conclude.
You are the least of goods, the worst of euils,
Your best are worse then men: your worst then diuels.

Babus second sonne.

Come let vs to our death: are we not blest?   1620
Our death will freedome from these creatures giue:
Those trouble quiet sowers of vnrest,
And this I vow that had I leaue to liue;
I would for euer leade a single life,
And neuer venter on a diuellish wife.

G   *Actus*

THE TRAGEDIE

Actus 4.   Scœna 7.

Herod and Salome.

Herod.

NAy, she shall die. Die quoth you, that she shall:
But for the meanes. The meanes! Me thinks tis
To finde a meanes to murther her withall,   (hard
Therefore I am resolu'd she shall be spar'd.
  Salom. Why? let her be beheaded. *Her.* That were
Thinke you that swords are miracles like you: (well,
Her skinne will eu'ry Curtlax edge refell,
And then your enterprise you well may rue.
What if the fierce Arabian notice take,
Of this your wretched weaponlesse estate:
They answere when we bid resistance make,
That *Mariams* skinne their fanchions did rebate.
Beware of this, you make a goodly hand,
If you of weapons doe depriue our Land.
  Sal. Why drowne her then. *Herod.* Indeed a sweet de-
Why? would not eu'ry Riuer turne her course   (uice,
Rather then doe her beautie preiudice?
And be reuerted to the proper sourse.
So not a drop of water should be found
In all Iudeas quondam firtill ground.
  Sal. Then let the fire deuoure her. *Her.* T'will not
Flame is from her deriu'd into my heart: (bee:
Thou nursest flame, flame will not murther thee,
My fairest *Mariam*, fullest of desert.   (die:
  Salom. Then let her liue for me. *Herod.* Nay, she shall
But can you liue without her? *Sal.* doubt you that?
  Herod. I'me sure I cannot, I beseech you trie:
I haue experience but I know not what.
  Salom. How should I try? *Her.* Why let my loue be
But if we cannot liue without her sight   (slaine,
                                                    Youl'e

OF MARIAM.

Youle finde the meanes to make her breathe againe,
Or elſe you will bereaue my comfort quite.   1660
   Sal. Oh I: I warrant you.   *Herod.* What is ſhe gone?
And gone to bid the world be ouerthrowne:
What? is her hearts compoſure hardeſt ſtone?
To what a paſſe are cruell women growne?
She is return'd already: haue you done?
Iſt poſſible you can command ſo ſoone?
A creatures heart to quench the flaming Sunne,
Or from the skie to wipe away the Moone.
   Salo. If *Mariam* be the Sunne and Moone, it is:
For I already haue commanded this.   (times. 1670
   Her. But haue you ſeene her cheek?   *Sal.* A thouſand
   Herod. But did you marke it too?   *Sal.* I very well.
   Herod. What iſt?   *Sal.* A Crimſon buſh, that euer limes
The ſoule whoſe foreſight doth not much excell.
   Herod. Send word ſhe ſhall not dye. Her cheek a buſh,
Nay, then I ſee indeed you markt it not.
   Sal. Tis very faire, but yet will neuer bluſh,
Though foule diſhonors do her forehead blot.
   Herod. Then let her die, tis very true indeed,
And for this fault alone ſhall *Mariam* bleed.   1680
   Sal. What fault my Lord?   *Herod.* What fault iſt? you
If you be ignorant I know of none,   (that aske:
To call her backe from death ſhall be your taske,
I'm glad that ſhe for innocent is knowne.
For on the brow of *Mariam* hangs a Fleece,
Whoſe ſlendereſt twine is ſtrong enough to binde
The hearts of Kings, the pride and ſhame of *Greece*,
Troy flaming *Helens* not ſo fairely ſhinde.
   Salom. Tis true indeed, ſhe layes them out for nets,
To catch the hearts that doe not ſhune a baite: 1690
Tis time to ſpeake: for *Herod* ſure forgets
That *Mariams* very treſſes hide deceit.
   Her. Oh doe they ſo? nay, then you doe but well,
Inſooth I thought it had beene haire:
Nets call you them? Lord, how they doe excell,
I neuer ſaw a net that ſhow'd ſo faire.

               G 2   But

THE TRAGEDIE

But haue you heard her speake? *Sal.* You know I haue.
  Her: And were you not amaz'd? *Sal.* No, not a whit.
  Her. Then t'was not her you heard, her life Ile saue,
For *Mariam* hath a world amazing wit.   1700
  Salo. She speaks a beautious language, but within
Her heart is false as powder: and her tongue
Doth but allure the auditors to sinne,
And is the instrument to doe you wrong.
  Herod. It may be so: nay, tis so: shee's vnchaste,
Her mouth will ope to eu'ry strangers eare:
Then let the executioner make haste,
Left she inchant him, if her words he heare.
Let him be deafe, left she do him surprise
That shall to free her spirit be assignde: 1710
Yet what boots deafenes if he haue his eyes,
Her murtherer must be both deafe and blinde.
For if he see, he needs must see the starres
That shine on eyther side of *Mariams* face:
Whose sweet aspect will terminate the warres,
Wherewith he should a soule so precious chafe.
Her eyes can speake, and in their speaking moue,
Oft did my heart with reuerence receiue
The worlds mandates. Pretty tales of loue
They vtter, which can humane bondage weaue.   1720
But shall I let this heauens modell dye?
Which for a small selfe-portraiture she drew:
Her eyes like starres, her forehead like the skie,
She is like Heauen, and must be heauenly true.
  Salom. Your thoughts do raue with doating on the
Her eyes are ebon hewde, and you'll confesse: (Queen,
A sable starre hath beene but seldome seene,
Then speake of reason more, of *Mariam* lesse.
  Herod. Your selfe are held a goodly creature heere,
Yet so vnlike my *Mariam* in your shape: 1730
That when to her you haue approached neere,
My selfe hath often tane you for an Ape.
And yet you prate of beautie: goe your waies,
You are to her a Sun-burnt Blackamore:
                          Your

OF MARIAM.

Your paintings cannot equall *Mariams* praise,
Her nature is so rich, you are so poore.
Let her be staide from death, for if she die;
We do we know not what to stop her breath:
A world cannot another *Mariam* buy,
Why stay you lingring? countermaund her death.   1740
  Salo. Then youle no more remember what hath past,
Sohemus loue, and hers shall be forgot:
Tis well in truth: that fault may be her last,
And she may mend, though yet she loue you not.
  Her: Oh God: tis true. *Sohemus:* earth and heau'n,
Why did you both conspire to make me curst:
In cousning me with showes, and proofes vneu'n?
She show'd the best, and yet did proue the worst.
Her show was such, as had our singing king
The holy *Dauid, Mariams* beautie seene: 1750
The *Hittits* had then felt no deadly sting,
Nor *Bethsabe* had neuer bene a Queene.
Or had his sonne the wisest man of men,
Whose fond delight did most consist in change:
Beheld her face, he had bene staid agen,
No creature hauing her, can wish to range.
Had *Asuerus* seene my *Mariams* brow,
The humble *Iewe*, she might haue walkt alone:
Her beautious vertue should haue staid below,
Whiles *Mariam* mounted to the Persian throne.   1760
But what auailes it all: for in the waight
She is deceitfull, light as vanitie:
Oh she was made for nothing but a bait,
To traine some haples man to miserie.
I am the haples man that haue bene trainde,
To endles bondage. I will see her yet:
Me thinkes I should discerne her if she fainde,
Can humane eyes be dazde by womans wit?
Once more these eyes of mine with hers shall meet,
Before the headsman doe her life bereaue: 1770
Shall I for euer part from thee my sweet?
Without the taking of my latest leaue.

G 3   *Salo:*

THE TRAGEDIE

Salo: You had as good refolue to faue her now,
Ile ftay her death, tis well determined:
For fure fhe neuer more will breake her vow,
Sohemus and *Iofephus* both are dead.

   Herod. She fhall not liue, nor will I fee her face,
A long heald wound, a fecond time doth bleed:
With *Iofeph* I remember her difgrace,
A fhamefull end enfues a fhamefull deed.   1780
Oh that I had not cald to minde anew,
The difcontent of *Mariams* wauering hart:
Twas you: you foule mouth'd *Ate*, none but you,
That did the thought hereof to me impart.
Hence from my fight, my blacke tormenter hence,
For hadft not thou made *Herod* vnfecure:
I had not doubted *Mariams* innocence,
But ftill had held her in my heart for pure.

   Salo: Ile leaue you to your paffion: tis no time
To purge me now, though of a guiltles crime.   (*Exit.* 1790

   Herod. Deftruction take thee: thou haft made   (my hart
As heauie as reuenge, I am fo dull,
Me thinkes I am not fenfible of fmart,
Though hiddious horrors at my bofome pull.
My head waies downwards: therefore will I goe
To try if I can fleepe away my woe.

Actus 4.   Scœna. 8.

Mariam.

AM I the *Mariam* that prefum'd fo much, (breath?
And deem'd my face muft needes preferue my   1800
I, I it was that thought my beautie fuch,
At it alone could countermaund my death.
Now death will teach me: he can pale afwell
A cheeke of rofes, as a cheeke leffe bright:
And dim an eye whofe fhine doth moft excell,
Affoone as one that cafts a meaner light.

                                              Had

OF MARIAM.

Had not my selfe against my selfe conspirde,
No plot: no aduersarie from without
Could *Herods* loue from *Mariam* haue retirde,
Or from his heart haue thrust my semblance out. 1810
The wanton Queene that neuer lou'd for loue,
False *Cleopatra*, wholly set on gaine:
With all her slights did proue: yet vainly proue,
For her the loue of *Herod* to obtaine.
Yet her allurements, all her courtly guile,
Her smiles, her fauours, and her smooth deceit:
Could not my face from *Herods* minde exile,
But were with him of lesse then little weight.
That face and person that in *Asia* late
For beauties Goddesse *Paphos* Queene was tane: 1820
That face that did captiue great *Iulius* fate,
That very face that was *Anthonius* bane.
That face that to be *Egipts* pride was borne,
That face that all the world esteem'd so rare:
Did *Herod* hate, despise, neglect, and scorne,
When with the same, he *Mariams* did compare.
This made that I improuidently wrought,
And on the wager euen my life did pawne:
Because I thought, and yet but truly thought,
That *Herods* loue could not from me be drawne. 1830
But now though out of time, I plainly see
It could be drawne, though neuer drawne from me:
Had I but with humilitie bene grac'te,
As well as faire I might haue prou'd me wise:
But I did thinke because I knew me chaste,
One vertue for a woman, might suffice.
That mind for glory of our sexe might stand,
Wherein humilitie and chastitie
Doth march with equall paces hand in hand,
But one if single seene, who setteth by? 1840
And I had singly one, but tis my ioy,
That I was euer innocent, though sower:
And therefore can they but my life destroy,
My Soule is free from aduersaries power.) *Enter Doris.*

You

THE TRAGEDIE

You Princes great in power, and high in birth,
Be great and high, I enuy not your hap:
Your birth muſt be from duſt: your power on earth,
In heau'n ſhall *Mariam* ſit in *Saraes* lap. (thither,
    Doris. I heau'n, your beautie cannot bring you 1850
Your ſoule is blacke and ſpotted, full of ſinne:
You in adultry liu'd nine yeare together,
And heau'n will neuer let adultry in.
    Mar: What art thou that doſt poore *Mariam* purſue?
Some ſpirit ſent to driue me to diſpaire:
Who ſees for truth that *Mariam* is vntrue,
If faire ſhe be, ſhe is as chaſte as faire.
    Doris. I am that *Doris* that was once belou'd,
Belou'd by *Herod*: *Herods* lawfull wife:
Twas you that *Doris* from his ſide remou'd,
And rob'd from me the glory of my life. 1860
    Mar: Was that adultry: did not Moſes ſay,
That he that being matcht did deadly hate:
Might by permiſſion put his wife away,
And take a more belou'd to be his mate?
    Doris. What did he hate me for: for ſimple truth?
For bringing beautious babes for loue to him:
For riches: noble birth, or tender youth,
Or for no ſtaine did *Doris* honour dim?
Oh tell me *Mariam*, tell me if you knowe,
Which fault of theſe made *Herod Doris* foe. 1870
Theſe thrice three yeares haue I with hands held vp,
And bowed knees faſt nailed to the ground:
Beſought for thee the dreggs of that ſame cup,
That cup of wrath that is for ſinners found.
And now thou art to drinke it: *Doris* curſe,
Vpon thy ſelfe did all this while attend,
But now it ſhall purſue thy children worſe.
    Mar: Oh *Doris* now to thee my knees I bend,
That hart that neuer bow'd to thee doth bow:
Curſe not mine infants, let it thee ſuffice, 1880
That Heau'n doth puniſhment to me allow.
Thy curſe is cauſe that guiltles *Mariam* dies.
                              Doris.

OF MARIAM.

Doris. Had I ten thousand tongues, and eu'ry tongue
Inflam'd with poisons power, and steept in gall:
My curses would not answere for my wrong,
Though I in cursing thee imployd them all.
Heare thou that didst mount *Gerarim* command,
To be a place whereon with cause to curse:
Stretch thy reuenging arme: thrust forth thy hand,
And plague the mother much: the children worse. 1890
Throw flaming fire vpon the baseborne heads
That were begotten in vnlawfull beds.
But let them liue till they haue sence to know
What tis to be in miserable state:
Then be their neerest friends their ouerthrow,
Attended be they by suspitious hate.
And *Mariam*, I doe hope this boy of mine
Shall one day come to be the death of thine. *Exit.*

  Mariam. Oh! Heauen forbid. I hope the world shall
This curse of thine shall be return'd on thee: (see, 1900
Now earth farewell, though I be yet but yong,
Yet I, me thinks, haue knowne thee too too long. *Exit.*

Chorus.

THe fairest action of our humane life,
  Is scorniug to reuenge an iniurie:
    For who forgiues without a further strife,
His aduersaries heart to him doth tie.
    And tis a firmer conquest truely sed,
    To winne the heart, then ouerthrow the head.

If we a worthy enemie doe finde, 1910
To yeeld to worth, it must be nobly done:
But if of baser mettall be his minde,
In base reuenge there is no honor wonne.
    Who would a worthy courage ouerthrow,
    And who would wrastle with a worthles foe?

THE TRAGEDIE

We say our hearts are great and cannot yeeld,
Because they cannot yeeld it proues them poore:
Great hearts are task't beyond their power, but seld
The weakest Lyon will the lowdest roare.
    Truths schoole for certaine doth this same allow,
    High hartednes doth sometimes teach to bow.

A noble heart doth teach a vertuous scorne,
To scorne to owe a dutie ouer-long:
To scorne to be for benefits forborne,
To scorne to lie, to scorne to doe a wrong.
    To scorne to beare an iniurie in minde,
    To scorne a free-borne heart slaue-like to binde.

But if for wrongs we needs reuenge must haue,
Then be our vengeance of the noblest kinde:
Doe we his body from our furie saue,
And let our hate preuaile against our minde?
    What can gainst him a greater vengeance bee,
    Then make his foe more worthy farre then hee?

Had *Mariam* scorn'd to leaue a due vnpaide,
Shee would to *Herod* then haue paid her loue:
And not haue bene by sullen passion swaide
To fixe her thoughts all iniurie aboue
    Is vertuous pride. Had *Mariam* thus bene prou'd,
    Long famous life to her had bene allowd.

Actus quintus. Scœna prima.

Nuntio.

WHen, sweetest friend, did I so farre offend
    Your heauenly selfe: that you my fault to quit

OF MARIAM.

Haue made me now relator of her end,
The end of beautie? Chaſtitie and wit,
Was none ſo haples in the fatall place,
But I, moſt wretched, for the Queene t'chuſe,
Tis certaine I haue ſome ill boding face
That made me culd to tell this luckles newes.
And yet no news to *Herod*: were it new,   1950
To him vnhappy t'had not bene at all:
Yet doe I long to come within his vew,
That he may know his wife did guiltles fall:
And heere he comes.   Your *Mariam* greets you well.

Enter Herod.

Herod. What? liues my *Mariam*? ioy, exceeding ioy.
She ſhall not die.   *Nun.* Heau'n doth your will repell.
Herod. Oh doe not with thy words my life deſtroy,
I prethy tell no dying-tale: thine eye
Without thy tongue doth tell but too too much: 1960
Yet let thy tongues addition make me die,
Death welcome, comes to him whoſe griefe is ſuch.
Nunti. I went amongſt the curious gazing troope,
To ſee the laſt of her that was the beſt:
To ſee if death had hart to make her ſtoope,
To ſee the Sunne admiring *Phœnix* neſt.
VVhen there I came, vpon the way I ſaw
The ſtately *Mariam* not debas'd by feare:
Her looke did ſeeme to keepe the world in awe,
Yet mildly did her face this fortune beare.   1970
Herod. Thou doſt vſurpe my right, my tongue was
To be the inſtrument of *Mariams* praiſe: (fram'd
Yet ſpeake: ſhe cannot be too often fam'd:
All tongues ſuffice not her ſweet name to raiſe.
Nun. But as ſhe came ſhe *Alexandra* met,

THE TRAGEDIE

Who did her death (fweet Queene) no whit bewaile,
But as if nature fhe did quite forget,
She did vpon her daughter loudly raile.
   Herod. Why ftopt you not her mouth? where had fhe
To darke that, that Heauen made fo bright?   (words 1980
Our facred tongue no *Epithite* affords,
To call her other then the worlds delight.
   Nun. Shee told her that her death was too too good,
And that already fhe had liu'd too long:
She faid, fhe fham'd to haue a part in blood
Of her that did the princely *Herod* wrong.   (glory,
   Herod. Bafe picke-thanke Diuell. Shame, twas all her
That fhe to noble *Mariam* was the mother:
But neuer fhall it liue in any ftorie
Her name, except to infamy ile fmother.   1990
What anfwere did her princely daughter make?
   Nun. She made no anfwere, but fhe lookt the while,
As if thereof fhe fcarce did notice take,
Yet fmilde, a dutifull, though fcornefull fmile.
   Her. Sweet creature, I that looke to mind doe call,
Full oft hath *Herod* bene amaz'd withall.
   Nun. Go on, fhe came vnmou'd with pleafant grace,
As if to triumph her arriuall were:
In ftately habite, and with cheefull face:
Yet eu'ry eye was moyft, but *Mariams* there.   2000
When iuftly oppofite to me fhe came,
She pickt me out from all the crue:
She beckned to me, cald me by my name,
For fhe my name, my birth, and fortune knew.
   Herod. What did fhe name thee? happy, happy man,
Wilt thou not euer loue that name the better?
But what fweet tune did this faire dying Swan
Afford thine eare: tell all, omit no letter.
   Nun. Tell thou my Lord, faid fhe.   *Her.* Mee, ment fhe
Ift true, the more my fhame: I was her Lord,   (mee? 2010
Were I not made her Lord, I ftill fhould bee:

                          But

OF MARIAM.

But now her name muſt be by me adord.
Oh ſay, what ſaid ſhe more? each word ſhe ſed
Shall be the food whereon my heart is fed.   (breath.
 Nun: Tell thou my Lord thou ſaw'ſt me looſe my
 Herod. Oh that I could that ſentence now controule.
 Nun. If guiltily eternall be my death,
 Her: I hold her chaſt eu'n in my inmoſt ſoule.
 Nun: By three daies hence if wiſhes could reuiue,
I know himſelfe would make me oft aliue.   2020
 Herod. Three daies: three houres, three minutes, not
A minute in a thouſand parts diuided,   (ſo much,
My penitencie for her death is ſuch,
As in the firſt I wiſht ſhe had not died.
But forward in thy tale. *Nun:* Why on ſhe went,
And after ſhe ſome ſilent praier had ſed:
She did as if to die ſhe were content,
And thus to heau'n her heau'nly ſoule is fled.
 Herod. But art thou ſure there doth no life remaine?
Iſt poſſible my *Mariam* ſhould be dead,   2030
Is there no tricke to make her breathe againe?
 Nun: Her body is diuided from her head   (art,
 Her: Why yet me thinkes there might be found by
Strange waies of cure, tis ſure rare things are don:
By an inuentiue head, and willing heart.
 Nun: Let not my Lord your fancies idlely run.
It is as poſſible it ſhould be ſeene,
That we ſhould make the holy Abraham liue,
Though he intomb'd two thouſand yeares had bene,
As breath againe to ſlaughtred *Mariam* giue.   2040
But now for more aſſaults prepare your eares,
 Herod. There cannot be a further cauſe of mone,
This accident ſhall ſhelter me from feares:
What can I feare? already *Mariams* gone.
Yet tell eu'n what you will: *Nun:* As I came by,
From *Mariams* death I ſaw vpon a tree,
A man that to his necke a cord did tie:

THE TRAGEDIE

Which cord he had defignd his end to bee.
When me he once difcern'd, he downwards bow'd,
And thus with fearefull voyce fhe cride alowd,   2050
Goe tell the King he trufted ere he tride,
I am the caufe that *Mariam* caufeles dide.
  Herod. Damnation take him, for it was the flaue
That faid fhe ment with poifons deadly force
To end my life that fhe the Crowne might haue:
Which tale did *Mariam* from her felfe diuorce.
Oh pardon me thou pure vnfpotted Ghoft,
My punifhment muft needes fufficient bee,
In miffing that content I valued moft:
Which was thy admirable face to fee.   2060
I had but one ineftimable Iewell,
Yet one I had no monarch had the like,
And therefore may I curfe my felfe as cruell:
Twas broken by a blowe my felfe did ftrike.
I gaz'd thereon and neuer thought me bleft,
But when on it my dazled eye might reft:
A pretious Mirror made by wonderous art,
I prizd it ten times dearer then my Crowne,
And laide it vp faft foulded in my heart:
Yet I in fuddaine choler caft it downe.   2070
And pafht it all to peeces: twas no foe,
That robd me of it; no *Arabian* hoft,
Nor no *Armenian* guide hath vfde me fo:
But *Herods* wretched felfe hath *Herod* croft.
She was my gracefull moytie, me accurft,
To flay my better halfe and faue my worft.
But fure fhe is not dead you did but ieft,
To put me in perplexitie a while,
Twere well indeed if I could fo be dreft:
I fee fhe is aliue, me thinkes you fmile.   2080
  Nun: If fainted *Abel* yet deceafed bee,
Tis certaine *Mariam* is as dead as hee.
  Her: Why then goe call her to me, bid her now

Put

OF MARIAM.

Put on faire habite, stately ornament:
And let no frowne oreshade her smoothest brow,
In her doth *Herod* place his whole content.
 Nun: Sheel come in stately weedes to please your (sence,
If now she come attirde in robe of heauen:
Remember you your selfe did send her hence,
And now to you she can no more be giuen. faire, 2090
 Herod. Shee's dead, hell take her murderers, she was
Oh what a hand she had, it was so white,
It did the whitenes of the snowe impaire:
I neuer more shall see so sweet a sight.
 Nun: Tis true, her hand was rare. *Her:* her hand? her (hands;
She had not singly one of beautie rare,
But such a paire as heere where *Herod* stands,
He dares the world to make to both compare.
Accursed *Salome*, hadst thou bene still,
My *Mariam* had bene breathing by my side: 2100
Oh neuer had I: had I had my will,
Sent forth command, that *Mariam* should haue dide.
But *Salome* thou didst with enuy vexe,
To see thy selfe out-matched in thy sexe:
Vpon your sexes forehead *Mariam* sat,
To grace you all like an imperiall crowne,
But you fond foole haue rudely pusht thereat,
And proudly puld your proper glory downe.
One smile of hers: Nay, not so much a : looke
Was worth a hundred thousand such as you, 2110
Iudea how canst thou the wretches brooke,
That robd from thee the fairest of the crew?
You dwellers in the now depriued land,
Wherein the matchles *Mariam* was bred:
Why graspe not each of you a sword in hand,
To ayme at me your cruell Soueraignes head.
Oh when you thinke of *Herod* as your King,
And owner of the pride of *Palestine*:
This act to your remembrance likewise bring,
         Tis

THE TRAGEDIE

Tis I haue ouerthrowne your royall line.
Within her purer vaines the blood did run,
That from her Grandam *Sara* she deriu'd,
Whose beldame age the loue of Kings hath wonne,
Oh that her issue had as long bene li'ud.
But can her eye be made by death obscure?
I cannot thinke but it must sparkle still:
Foule sacriledge to rob those lights so pure,
From out a Temple made by heau'nly skill.
I am the Villaine that haue done the deed,
The cruell deed, though by anothers hand,
My word though not my sword made *Mariam* bleed,
Hircanus Grandchild did at my command.
That *Mariam* that I once did loue so deare,
The partner of my now detested bed,
Why shine you sun with an aspect so cleare?
I tell you once againe my *Mariams* dead.
You could but shine, if some *Egiptian* blows,
Or *Æthiopian* doudy lose her life:
This was, then wherefore bend you not your brows,
The King of *Iuries* faire and spotles wife.
Denie thy beames, and *Moone* refuse thy light,
Let all the starres be darke, let *Iuries* eye
No more distinguish which is day and night:
Since her best birth did in her bosome die.
Those fond Idolaters the men of *Greece*,
Maintaine these orbes are safely gouerned:
That each within themselues haue Gods a peece,
By whom their stedfast course is iustly led.
But were it so, as so it cannot bee,
They all would put their mourning garments on:
Not one of them would yeeld a light to mee,
To me that is the cause that *Mariams* gon.
For though they faine their *Saturne* melancholy,
Of sowre behauiours, and of angry moode:
They faine him likewise to be iust and holy,

And

OF MARIAM.

And iustice needes must seeke reuenge for blood.
Their *Ioue*, if *Ioue* he were, would sure desire,
To punish him that slew so faire a lasse:
For *Lædaes* beautie set his heart on fire,
Yet she not halfe so faire as *Mariam* was.   2160
And *Mars* would deeme his *Venus* had bene slaine,
Sol to recouer her would neuer sticke:
For if he want the power her life to gaine:
Then Physicks God is but an Empericke.
The Queene of loue would storme for beauties sake,
And *Hermes* too, since he bestow'd her wit,
The nights pale light for angrie griefe would shake,
To see chast *Mariam* die in age vnfit.
But oh I am deceiu'd, she past them all
In euery gift, in euery propertie: 2170
Her Excellencies wrought her timeles fall,
And they reioyc'd, not grieu'd to see her die.
The *Paphian* Goddesse did repent her wast,
When she to one such beautie did allow:
Mercurius thought her wit his wit surpast,
And *Cinthia* enui'd *Mariams* brighter brow.
But these are fictions, they are voyd of sence,
The *Greekes* but dreame, and dreaming falsehoods tell:
They neither can offend nor giue defence,
And not by them it was my *Mariam* fell.   2180
If she had bene like an *Egiptian* blacke,
And not so faire, she had bene longer liude:
Her ouerflow of beautie turned backe,
And drownde the spring from whence it was deriude.
Her heau'nly beautie twas that made me thinke
That it with chastitie could neuer dwell:
But now I see that heau'n in her did linke,
A spirit and a person to excell.
Ile muffle vp my selfe in endles night,
And neuer let mine eyes behold the light.   2190
Retire thy selfe vile monster, worse then hee

THE TRAGEDIE

That ſtaind the virgin earth with brothers blood,
Still in ſome vault or denne incloſed bee,
Where with thy teares thou maiſt beget a flood,
Which flood in time may drowne thee: happie day
When thou at once ſhalt die and finde a graue,
A ſtone vpon the vault, ſome one ſhall lay,
Which monument ſhall an inſcription haue.
And theſe ſhall be the words it ſhall containe,
Heere Herod *lies, that hath his* Mariam *ſlaine.*   2200

Chorus.

WHo euer hath beheld with ſteadfaſt eye,
  The ſtrange euents of this one onely day:
    How many were deceiu'd? How many die,
That once to day did grounds of ſafetie lay?
  It will from them all certaintie bereue,
  Since twice ſixe houres ſo many can deceiue.

This morning *Herod* held for ſurely dead,
And all the *Iewes* on *Mariam* did attend:
And *Conſtabarus* riſe from *Saloms* bed,   2210
And neither dreamd of a diuorce or end.
  Pheroras ioyd that he might haue his wife,
  And *Babus* ſonnes for ſafetie of their life.

To night our *Herod* doth aliue remaine,
The guiltles *Mariam* is depriu'd of breath:
Stout *Conſtabarus* both diuorſt and ſlaine,
The valiant ſonnes of *Baba* haue their death.
  Pheroras ſure his loue to be bereft,
  If *Salome* her ſute vnmade had left.

Herod this morning did expect with ioy,   2220
To ſee his *Mariams* much beloued face:
And yet ere night he did her life deſtroy,

And

OF MARIAM.

And surely thought she did her name disgrace.
   Yet now againe so short do humors last,
   He both repents her death and knowes her chast.

Had he with wisedome now her death delaide,
He at his pleasure might command her death:
But now he hath his power so much betraide,
As all his woes cannot restore her breath.
   Now doth he strangely lunatickly raue,
   Because his *Mariams* life he cannot saue.

This daies euents were certainly ordainde,
To be the warning to posteritie:
So many changes are therein containde,
So admirablie strange varietie.
   This day alone, our sagest *Hebrewes* shall
   In after times the schoole of wisedome call.

FINIS.

THE TRAGEDY OF MARIAM 1613.

The copy of *Mariam* formerly in the Huth collection is not the only one which contains the dedicatory sonnet and list of characters. Another, it appears, is in the possession of Mr. W. A. White of New York, who has most kindly supplied the General Editor with photographs of the additional leaf. In view of the fact that so far as is known the only copies of this are now in America, it has been thought well to reproduce the two pages in collotype as well as issuing a type facsimile of them by way of supplement to the Society's reprint of the play. Mr. White's copy was bought from a London bookseller in 1890.

It will be observed as regards the sonnet that Hazlitt's reprint in *Notes and Queries*, while not quite accurate in details, is essentially faithful to the original. As regards 'The names of the Speakers' now reprinted for the first time, it will be noticed that the list has been compiled by some one possessing at best a superficial acquaintance with the play. Thus Antipater is said to be Herod's son by Salome instead of by Doris, Silleus' name is misprinted 'Sillius', while the abbreviation 'Bu.' is taken as representing the name of 'another Messenger', whereas in fact it almost certainly stands for 'Butler'.

ERRATUM.

Mariam, l. 1451. In some copies of the reprint an 'I' appears at the beginning of this line before the word 'would'. In the original there is no 'I', only a blank space. See note in the List of Doubtful Readings.

TO DIANAES
EARTHLIE DEPVTESSE,
and my worthy Sister, Mistris
Elizabeth Carye.

WHen cheerfull *Phœbus* his full course hath run,
His sisters fainter beames our harts doth cheere:
So your faire Brother is to mee the Sunne,
And you his Sister as my Moone appeere.

You are my next belou'd, my second Friend,
For when my *Phœbus* absence makes it Night,
Whilst to th' *Antipodes* his beames do bend,
From you my *Phœbe*, shines my second Light.

Hee like to *SOL*, cleare-sighted, constant, free,
You *LVNA*-like, vnspotted, chast, diuine:
Hee shone on *Sicily*, you destin'd bee,
T'illumine the now obscurde *Palestine*.
My first was consecrated to *Apollo*,
My second to *DIANA* now shall follow.

E. C.

The names of the Speakers.

Herod, King of *Iudea.*
Doris, his first Wife.
Mariam, his second Wife.
Salome, Herods Sister.
Antipater his sonne by *Salome.*
Alexandra, Mariams mother.
Silleus, Prince of *Arabia.*
Constabarus, husband to *Salome.*
Phæroras, Herods Brother.
Graphina, his Loue.
Babus first Sonne.
Babus second Sonne.
Annanell, the high Priest.
Sohemus, a Counseller to *Herod.*
Nuntio.
Bu. another Messenger.
Chorus, a Companie of *Iewes.*

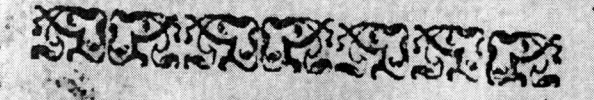

The

TO DIANAES
EARTHLIE DEPVTESSE,
and my worthy Sister, Mistris Elizabeth Carye.

WHen cheerful *Phœbus* his full course hath run,
His sisters fainter beams our harts doth cheere:
So your faire Brother is to mee the Sunne,
And you his Sister as my Moone appeere.

You are my next belou'd, my second Friend,
For when my *Phœbus* absence makes it Night,
Whilst to th'*Antipodes* his beames do bend,
From you my *Phœbe*, shines my second Light.

Hee like to SOL, cleare-sighted, constant, free,
You LVNA-like, vnspotted, chast, diuine:
Hee shone on *Sicily*, you destin'd bee,
T'illumine the now obscurde *Palestine*.
My first was consecrated to *Apollo*,
My second to DIANA now shall follow.

E. C.

The names of the Speakers.

Herod, King of Iudea.
Doris, his first Wife.
Mariam, his second Wife.
Salome, Herods Sister.
Antipater his sonne by Salome.
Alexandra, Mariams mother.
Sillius, Prince of Arabia.
Constabarus, husband to Salome.
Phæroras, Herods Brother.
Graphina, his Loue.
Babus first Sonne.
Babus second Sonne.
Annanell, the high Priest.
Sohemus, a Counsellor to Herod.
Nuntio.
Bu. another Messenger.
Chorus, a Companie of Iewes.

The